Adult Coloring Book

Strees Relieving Mandala Designs

Volume I

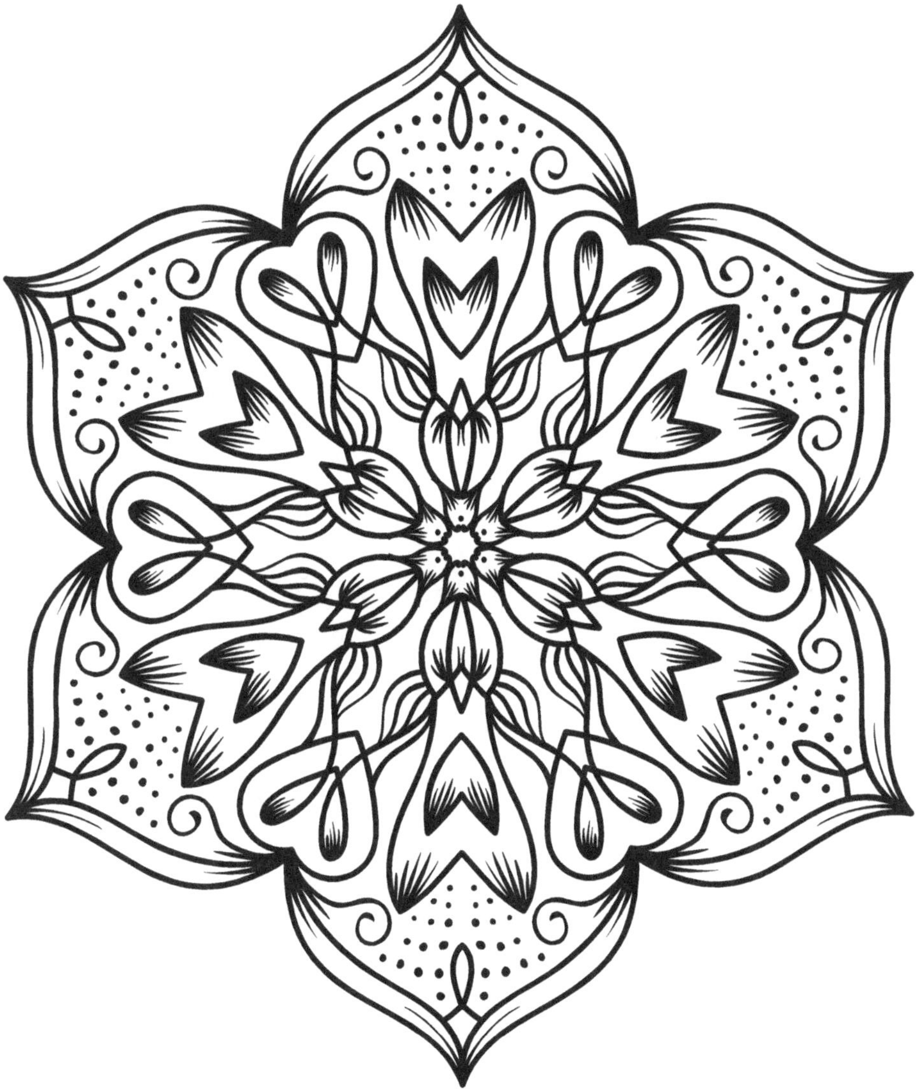

Creaty Style

www.creatystyle.com

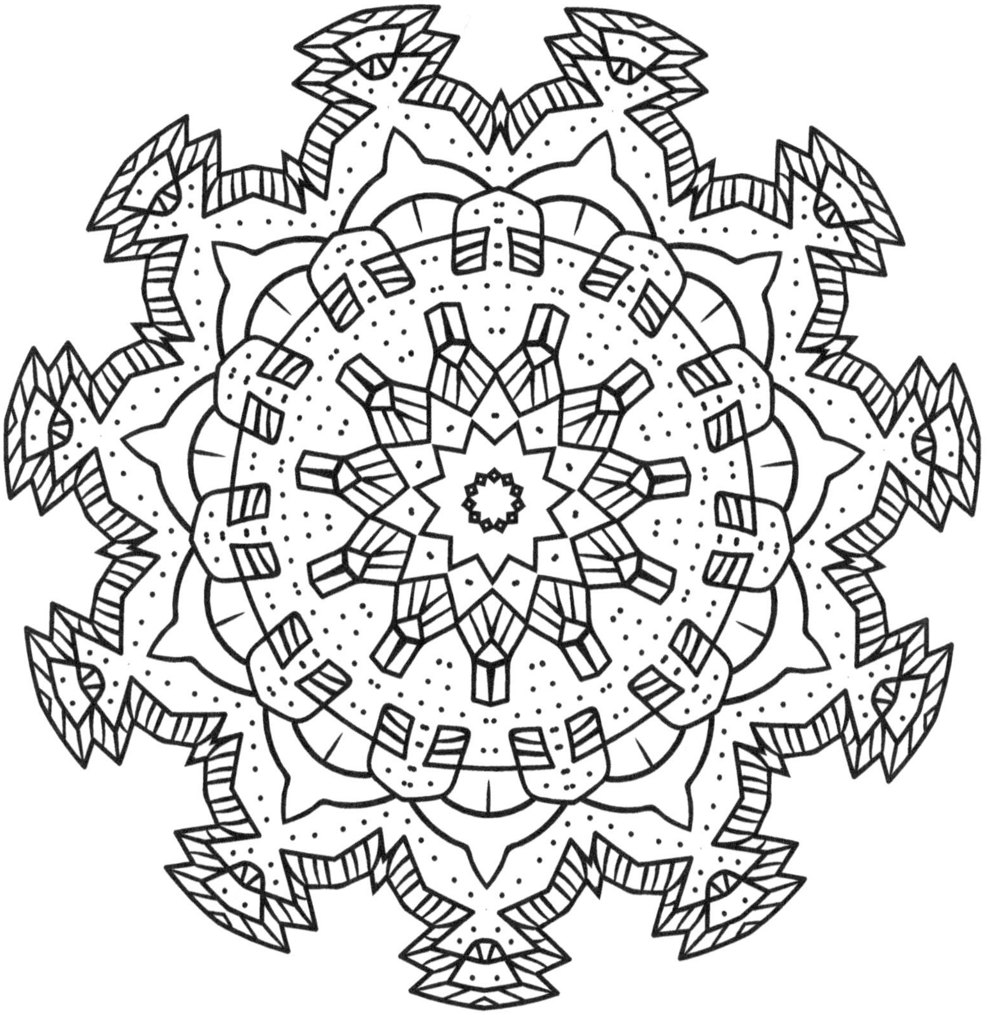

This Coloring Book Belongs to:

____

Color Test Page

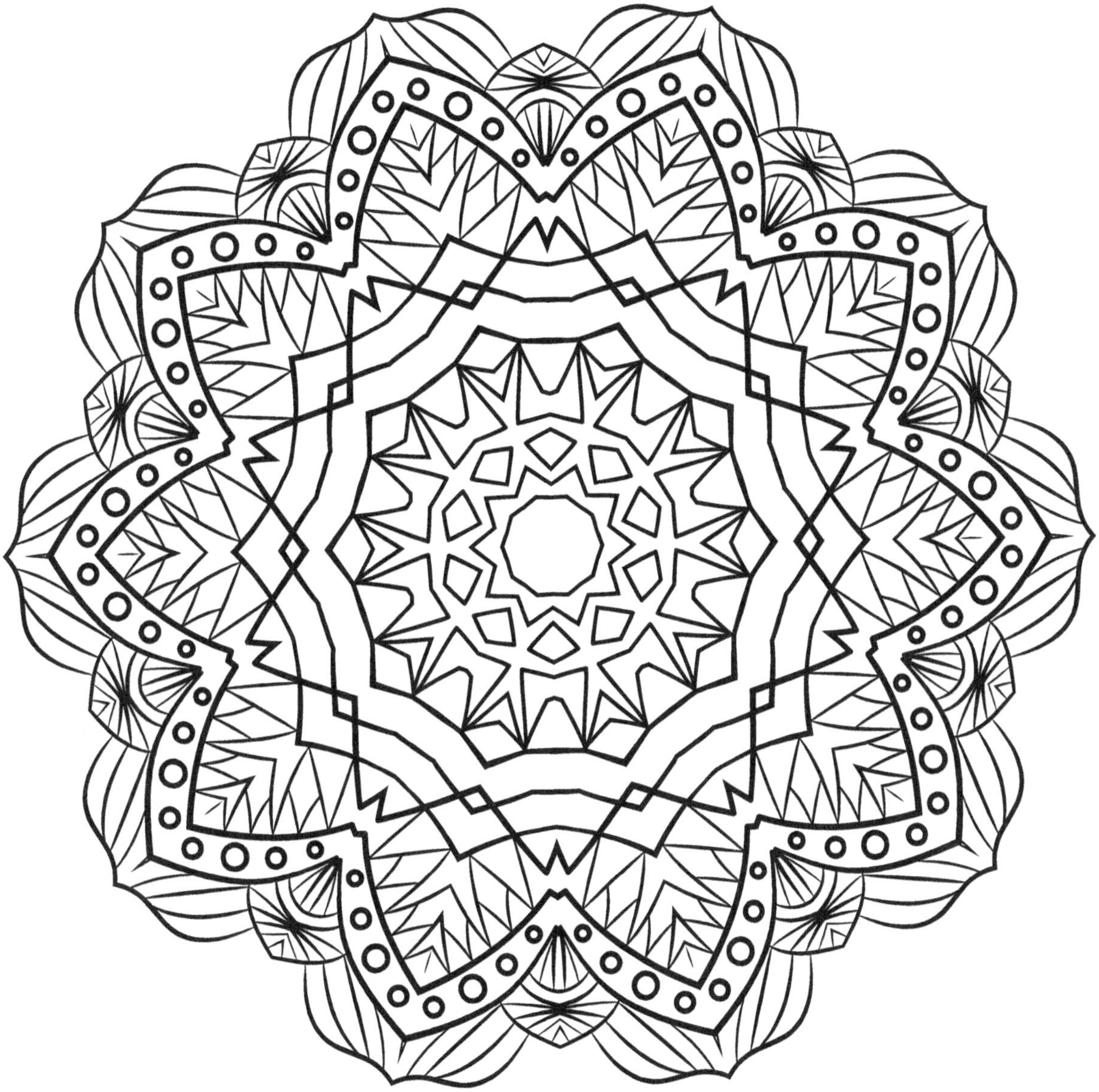

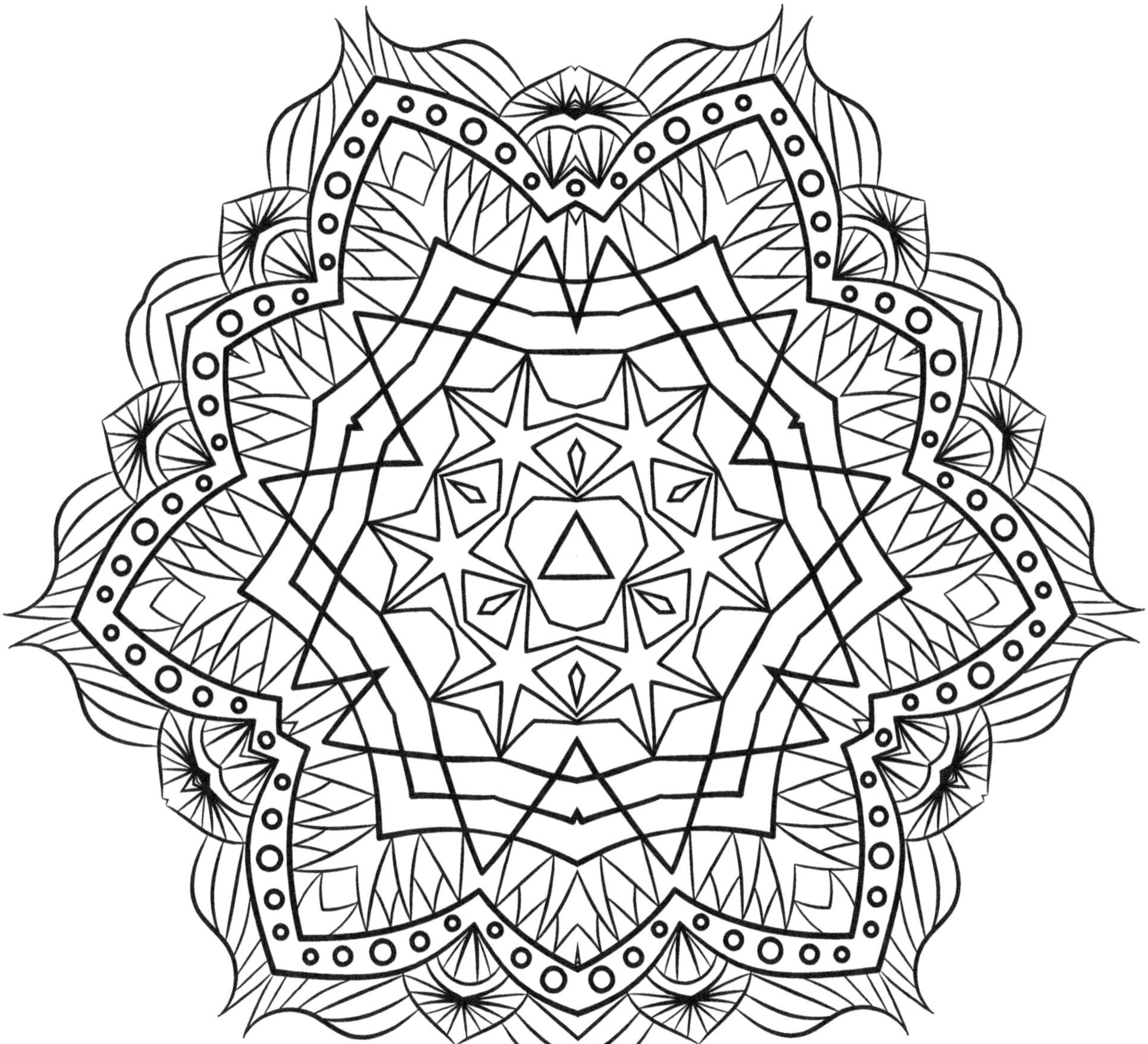

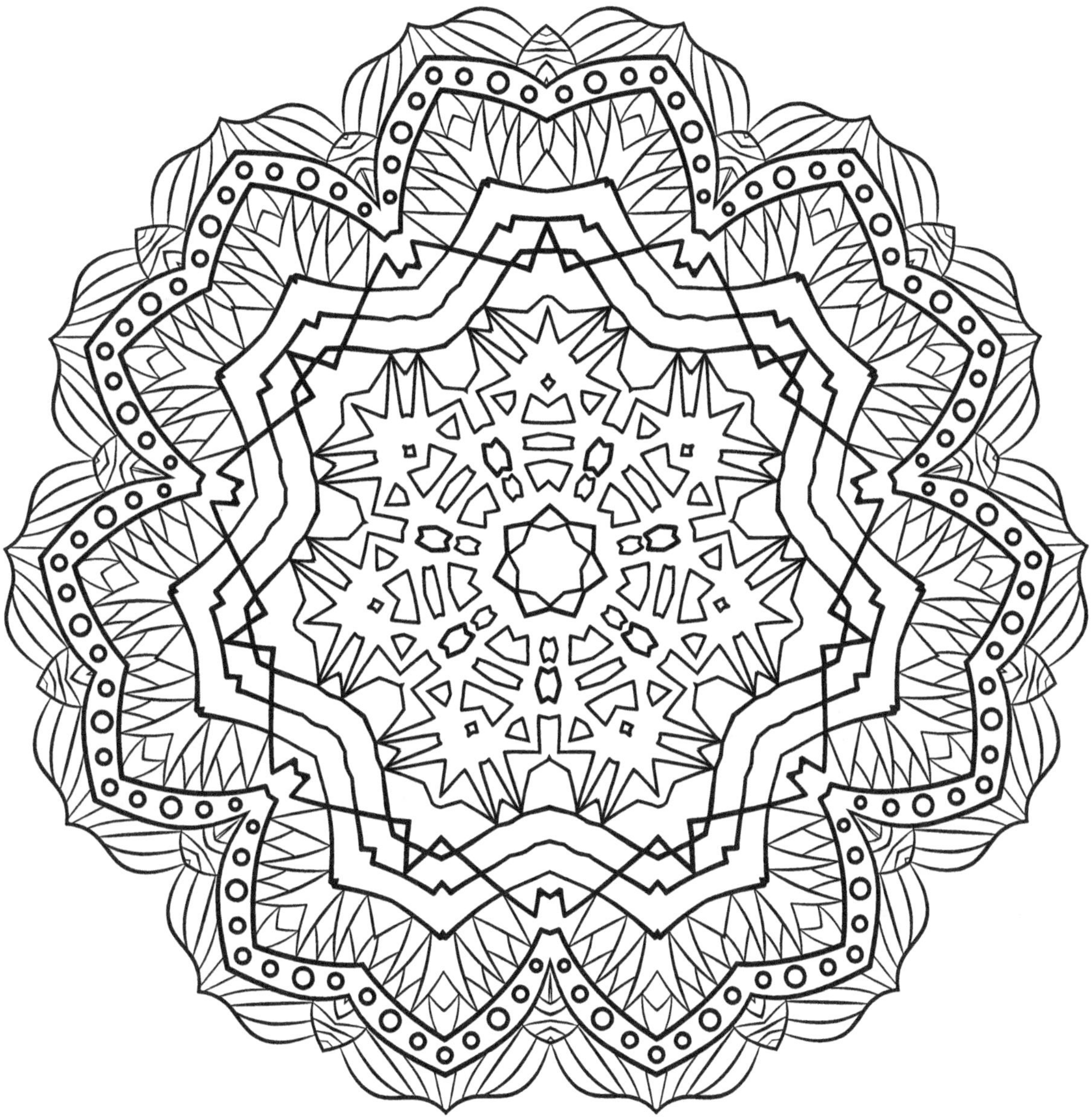

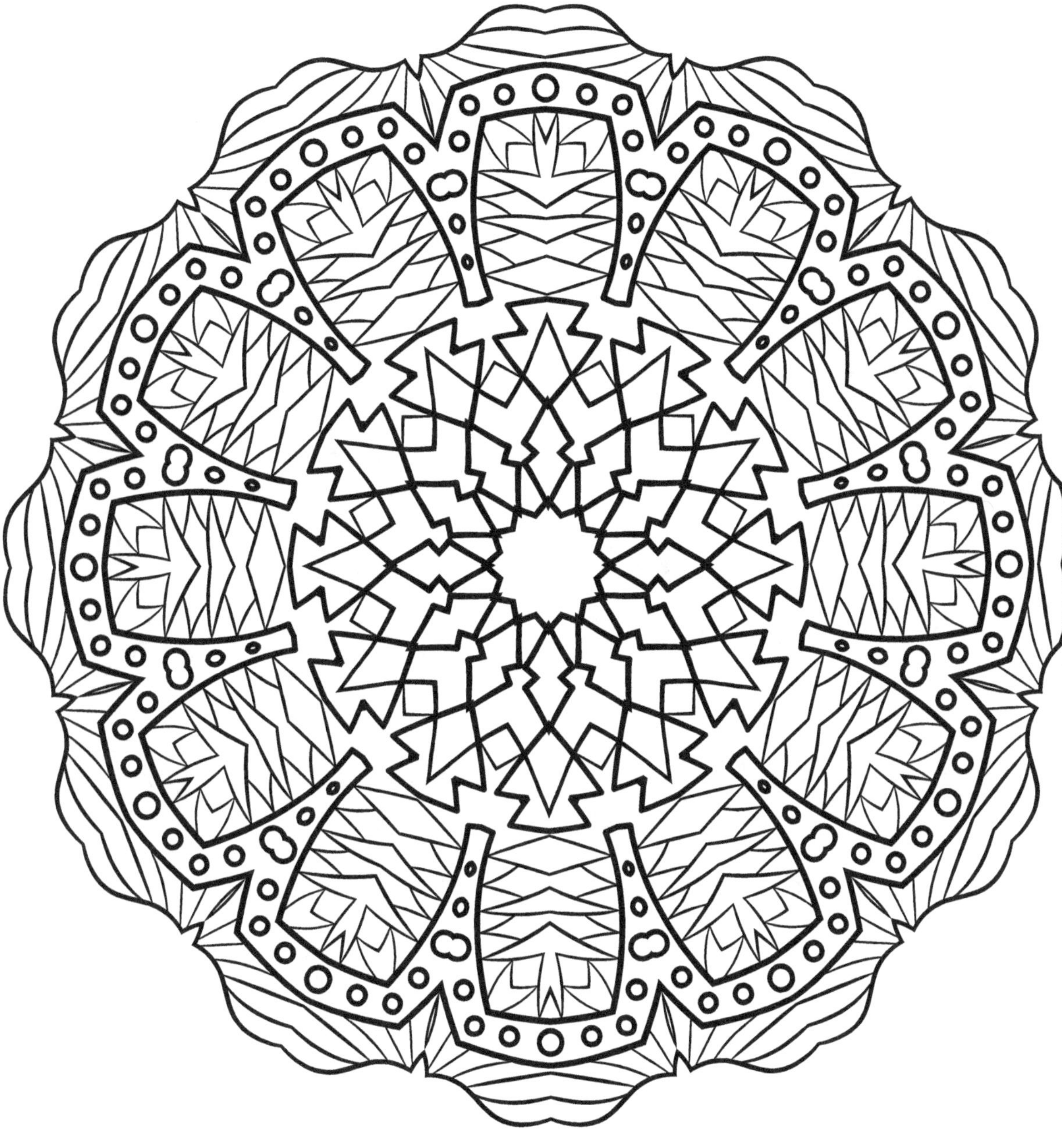

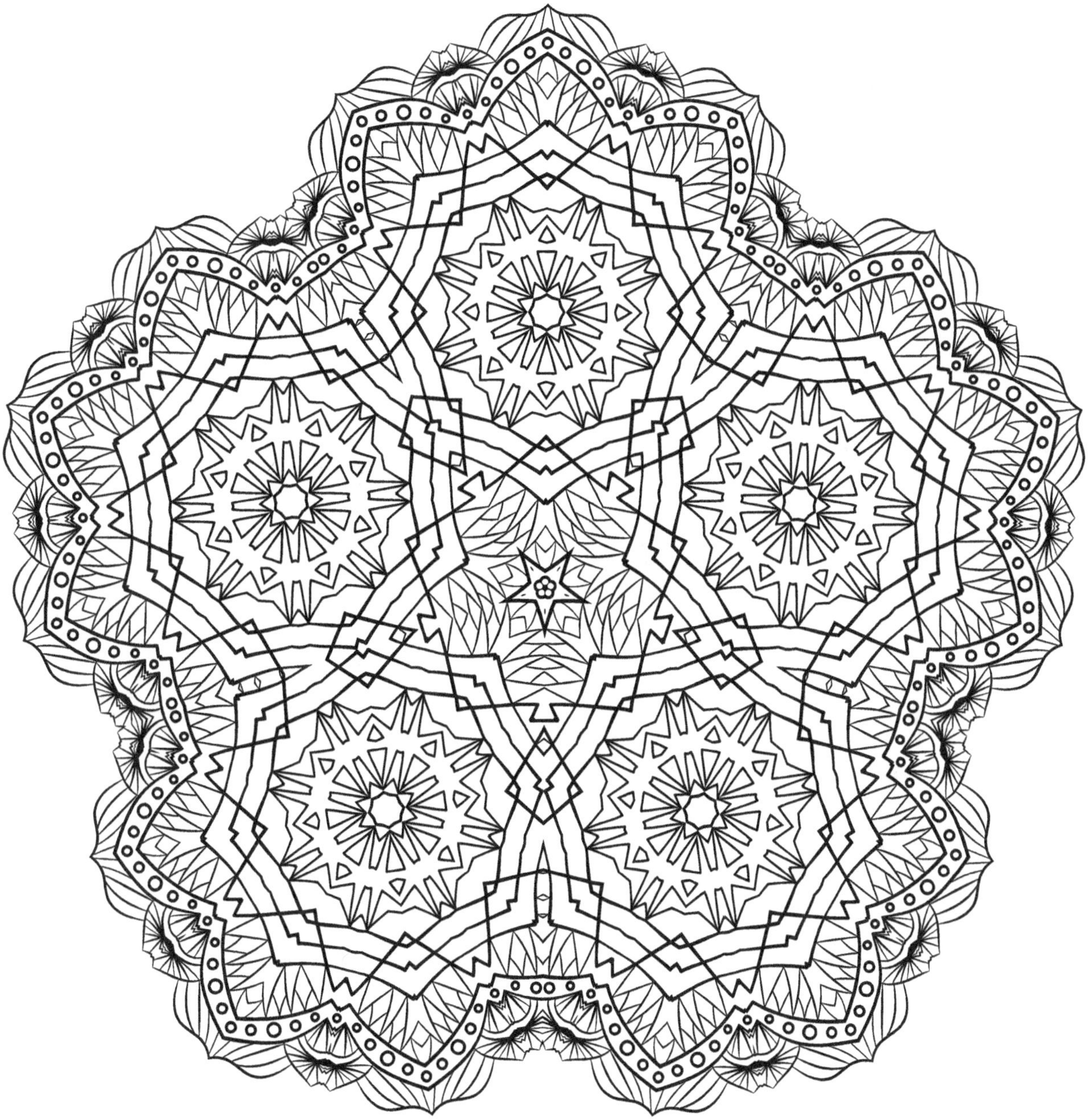

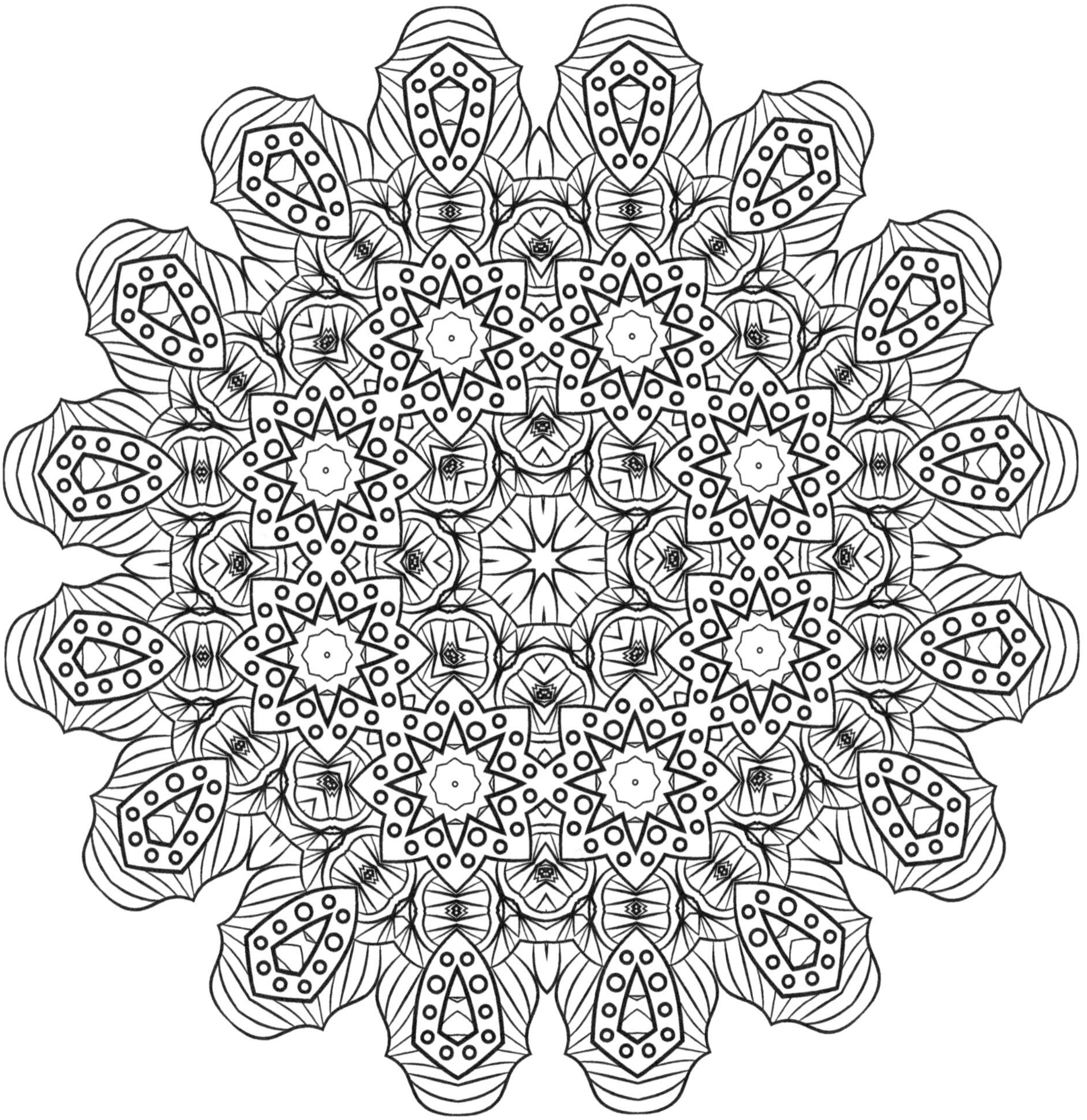

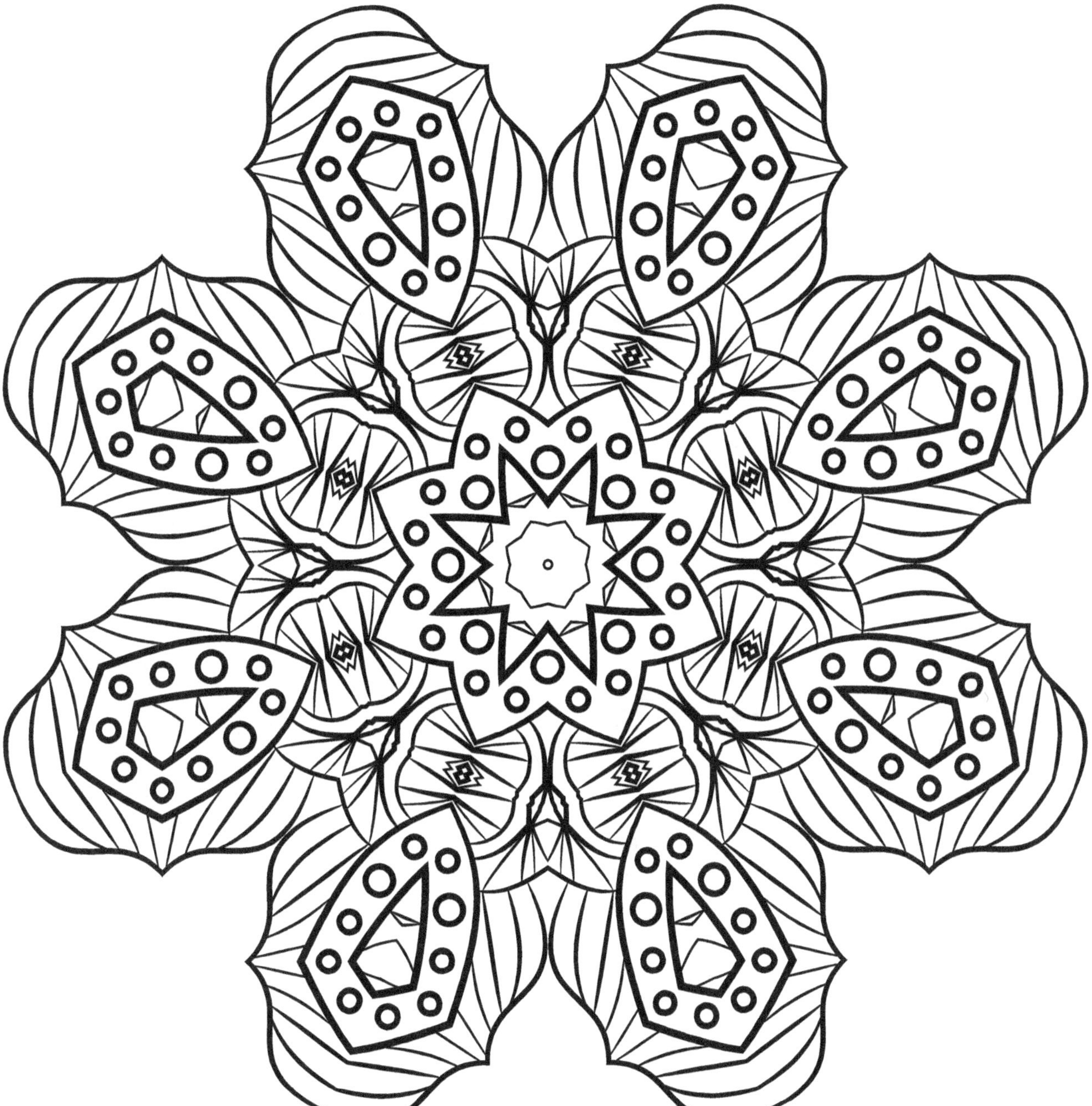

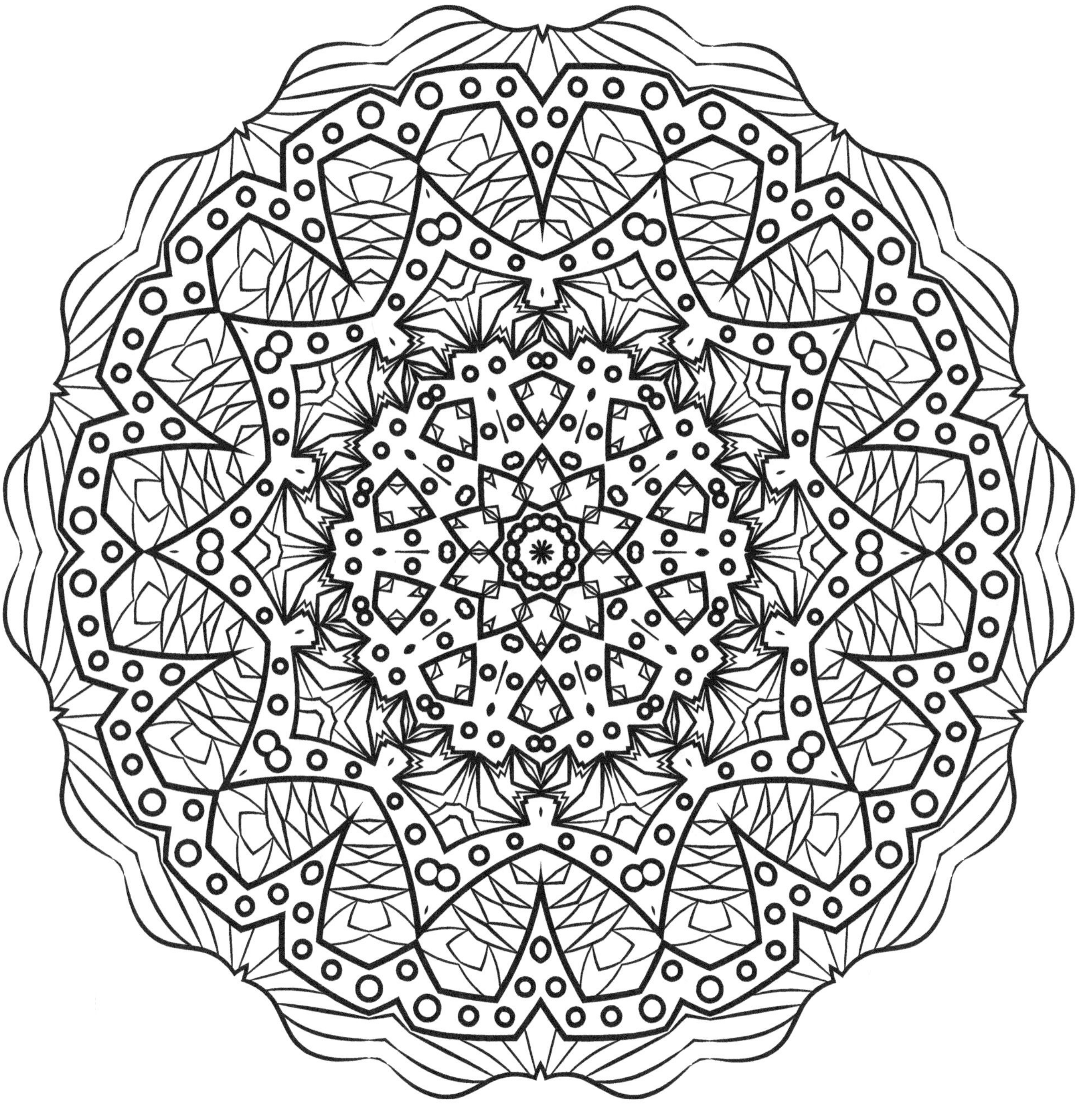

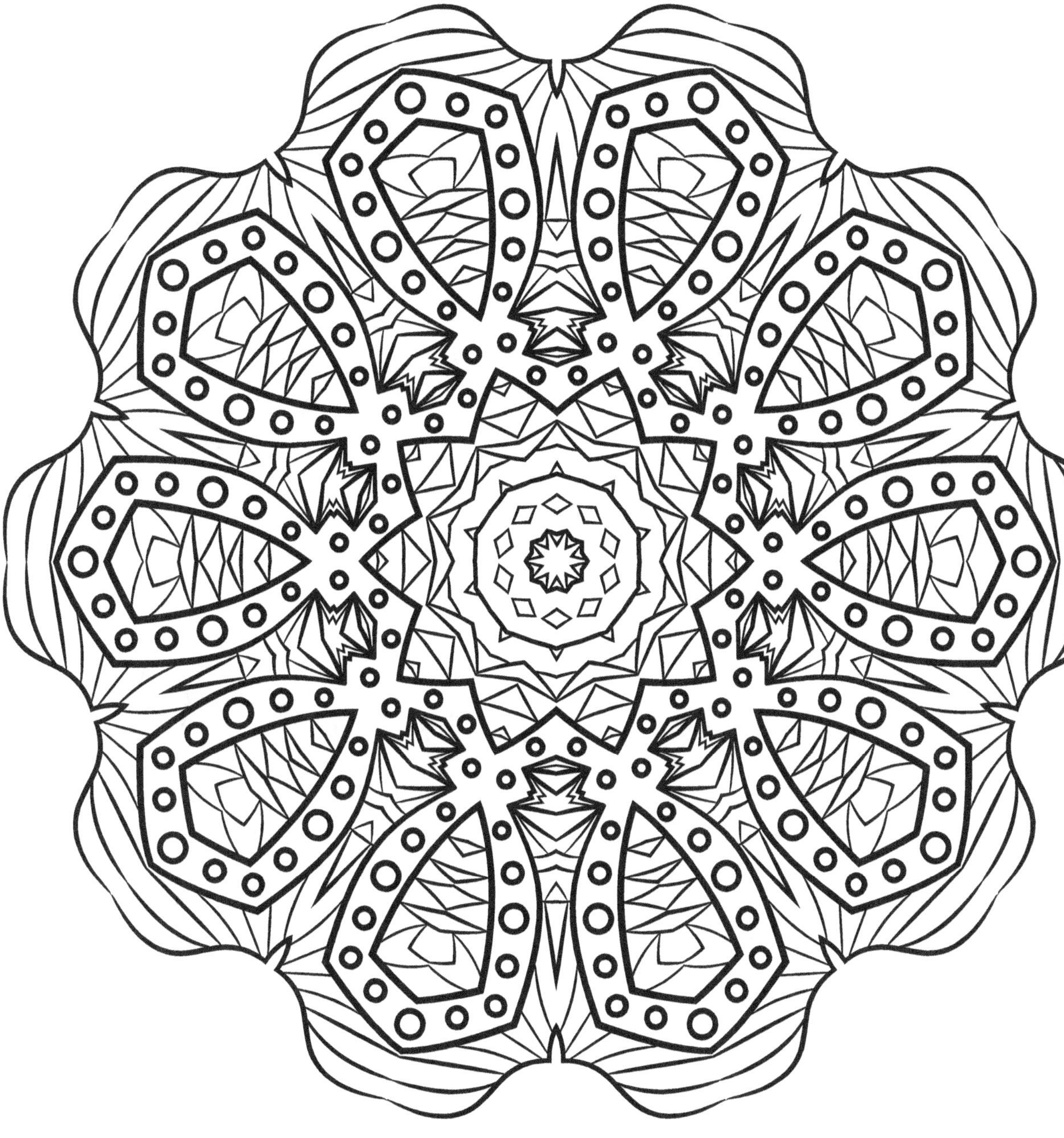

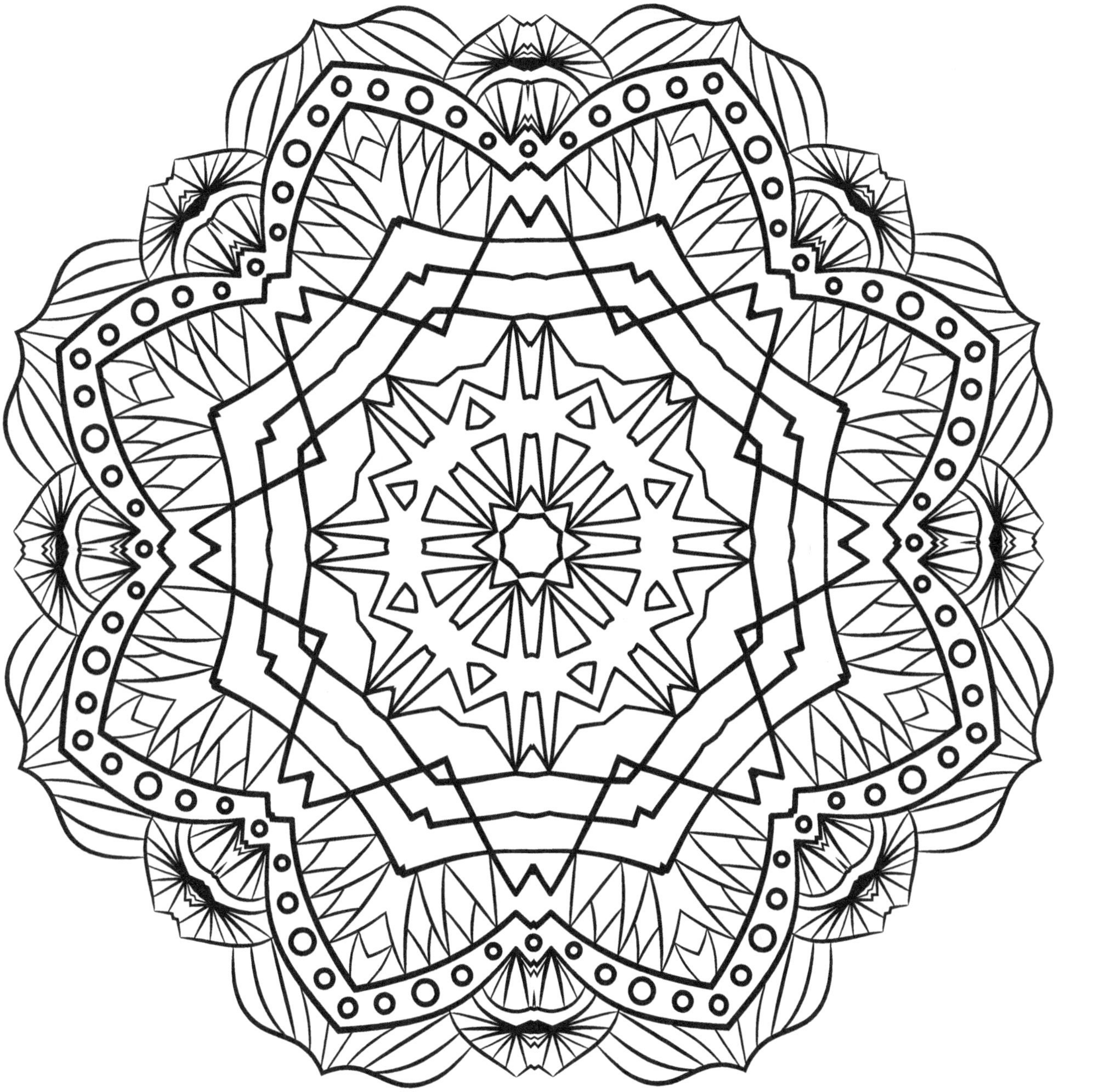

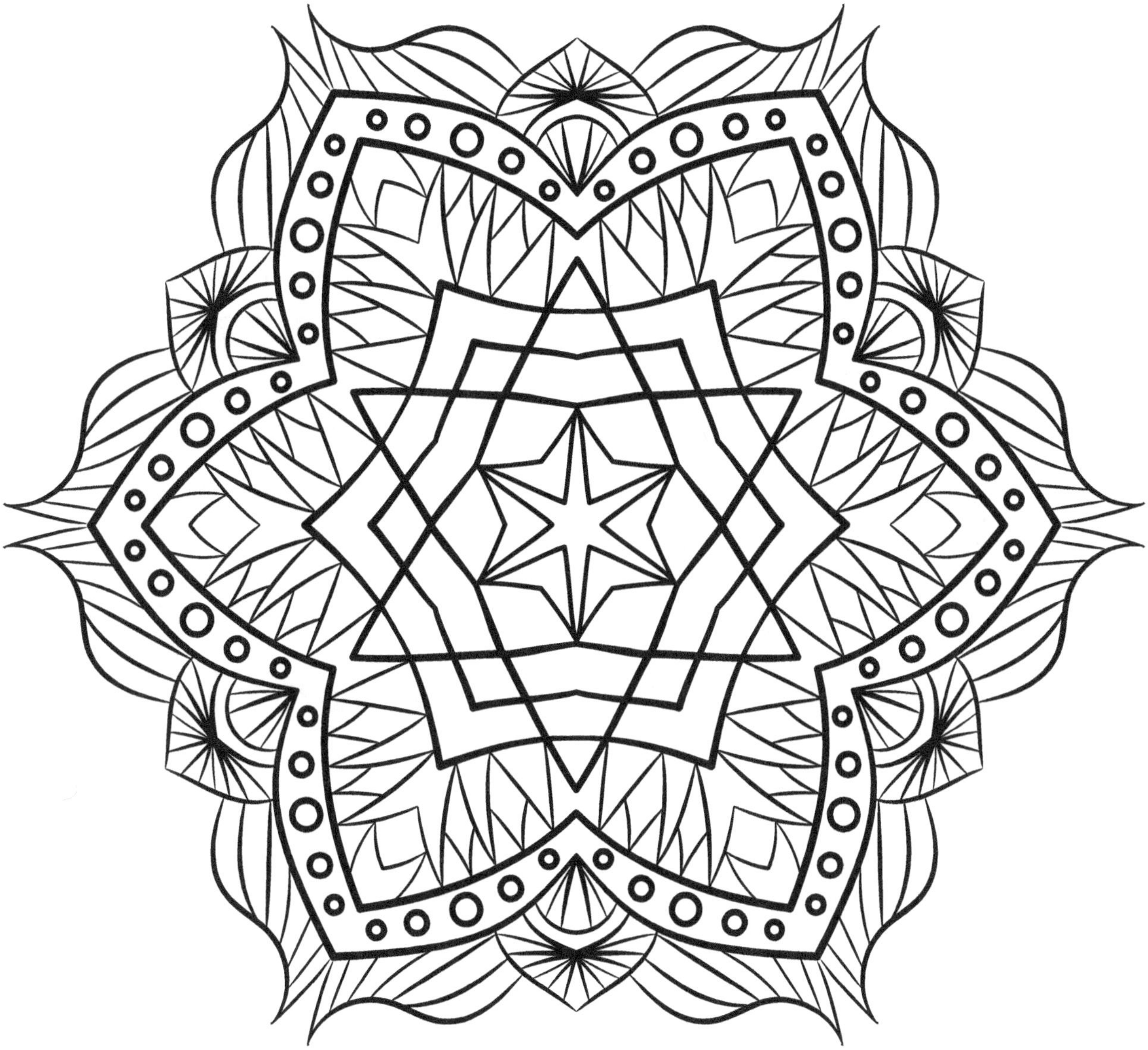

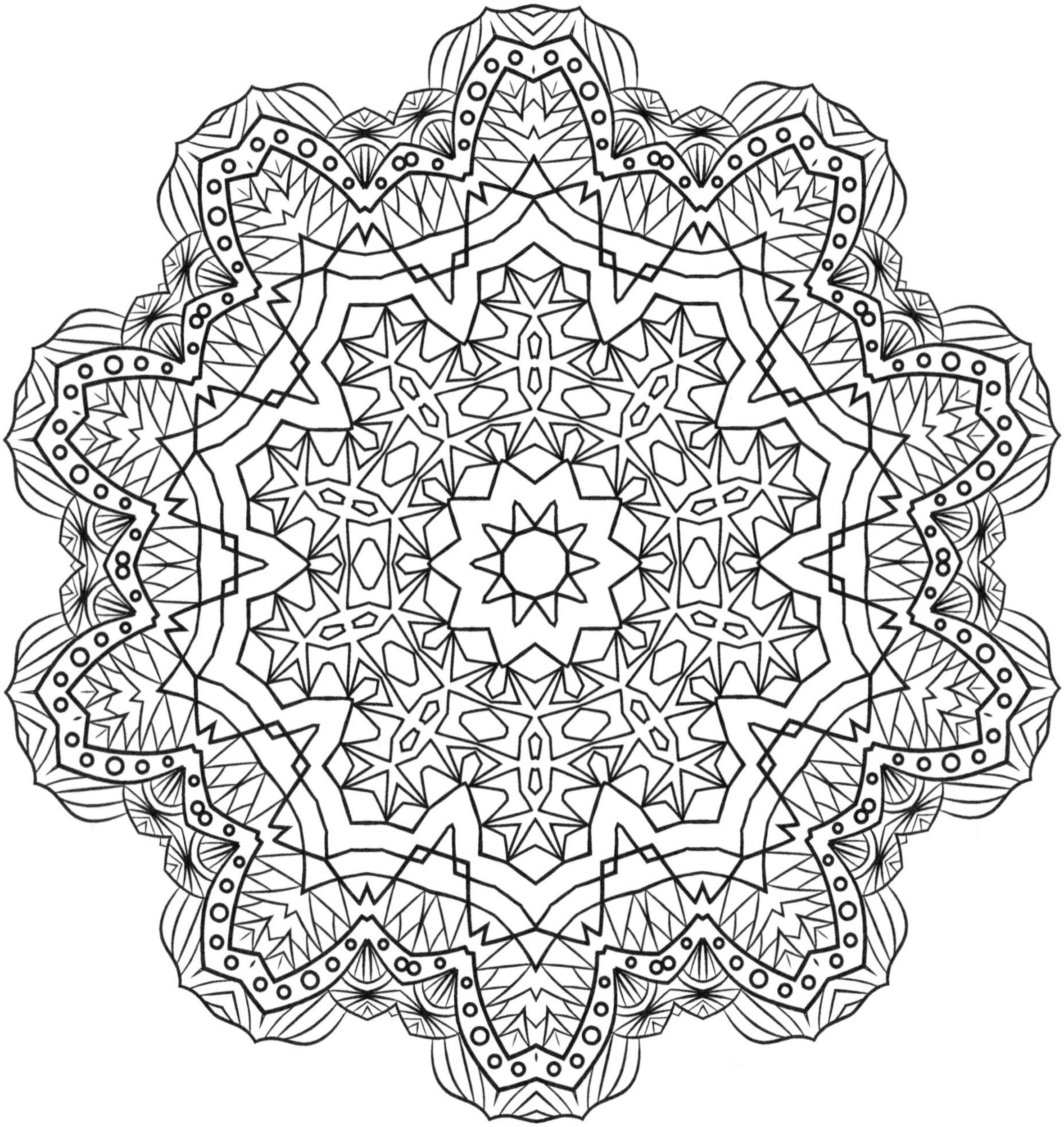

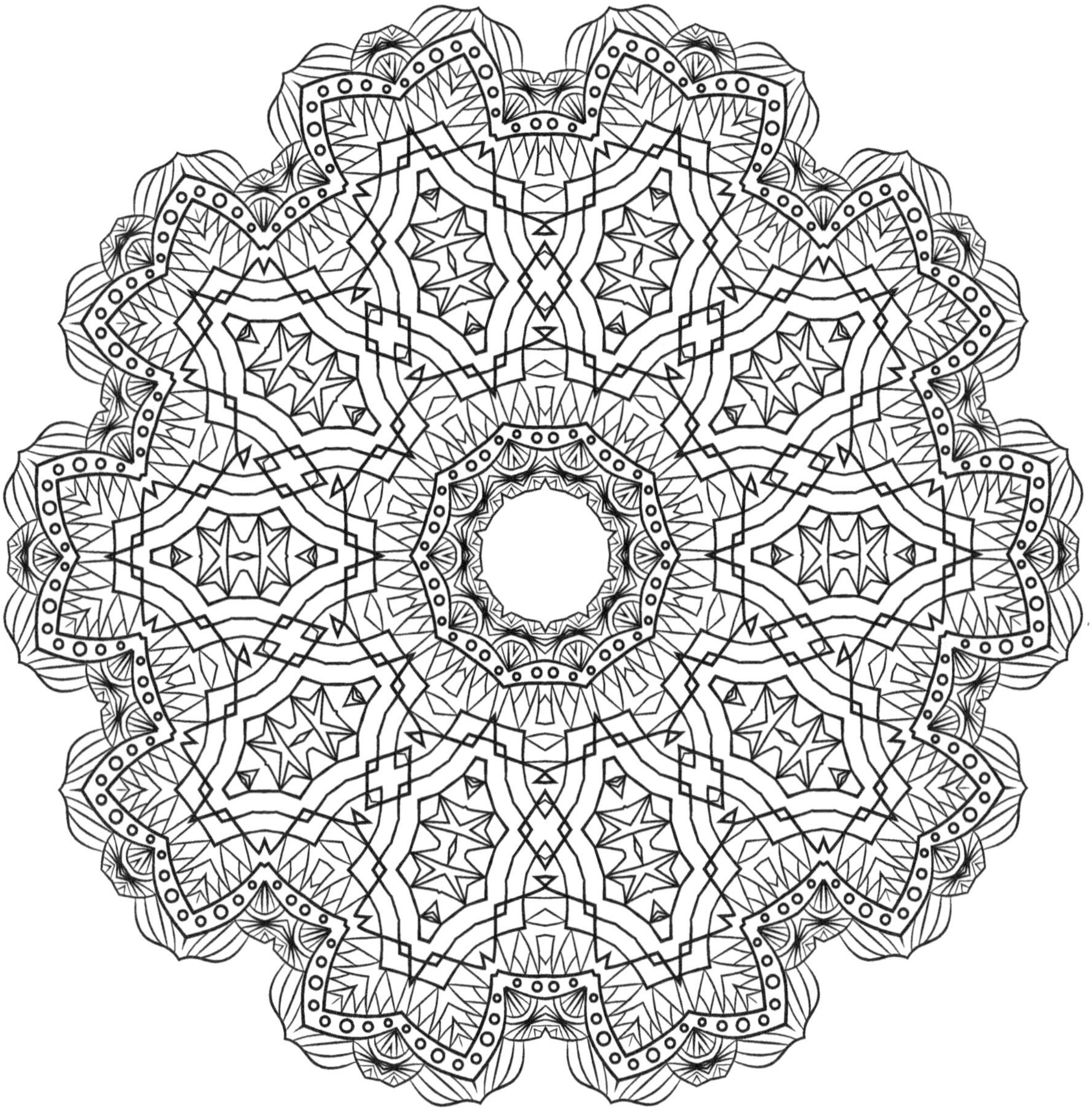

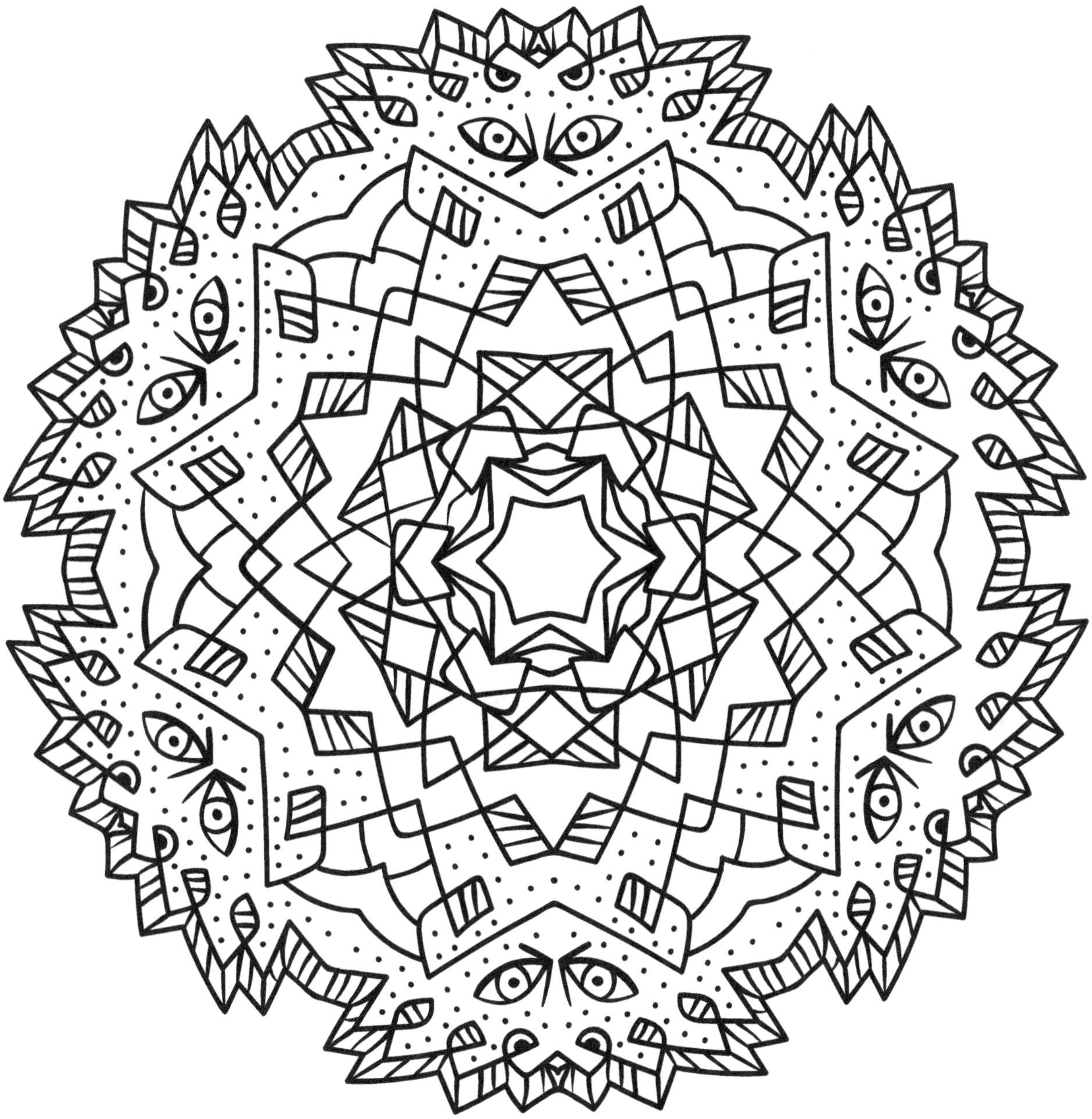

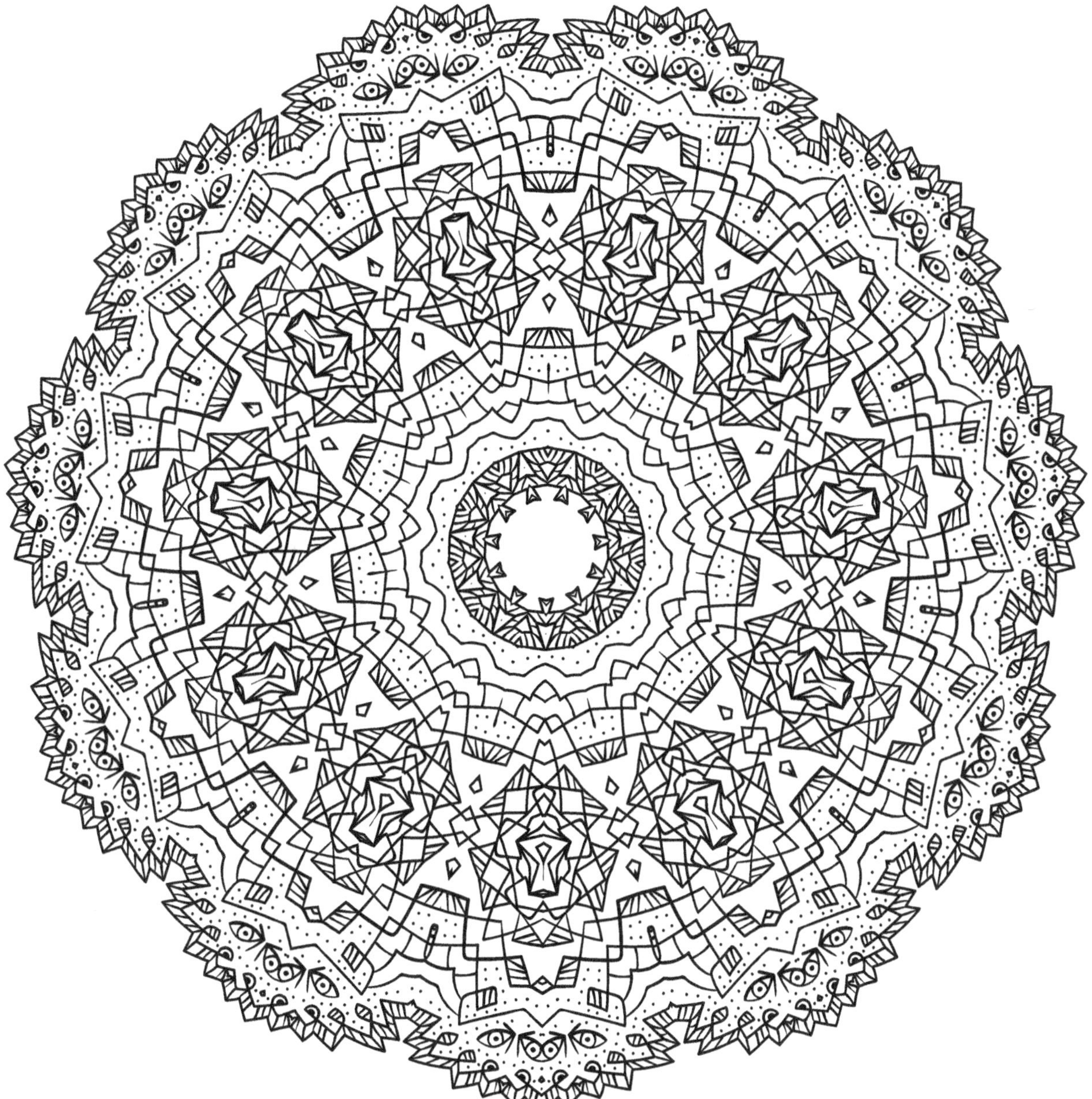

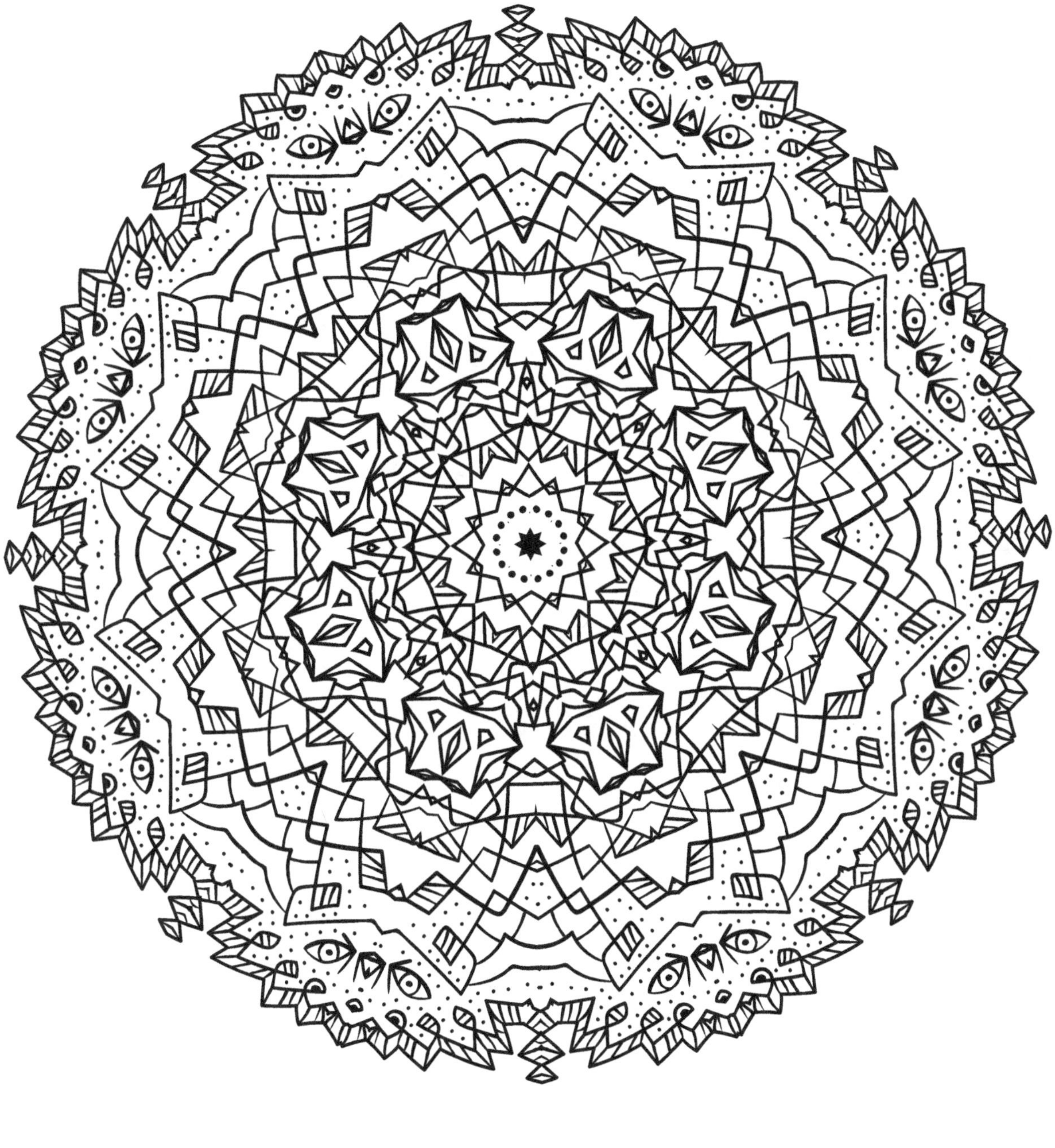

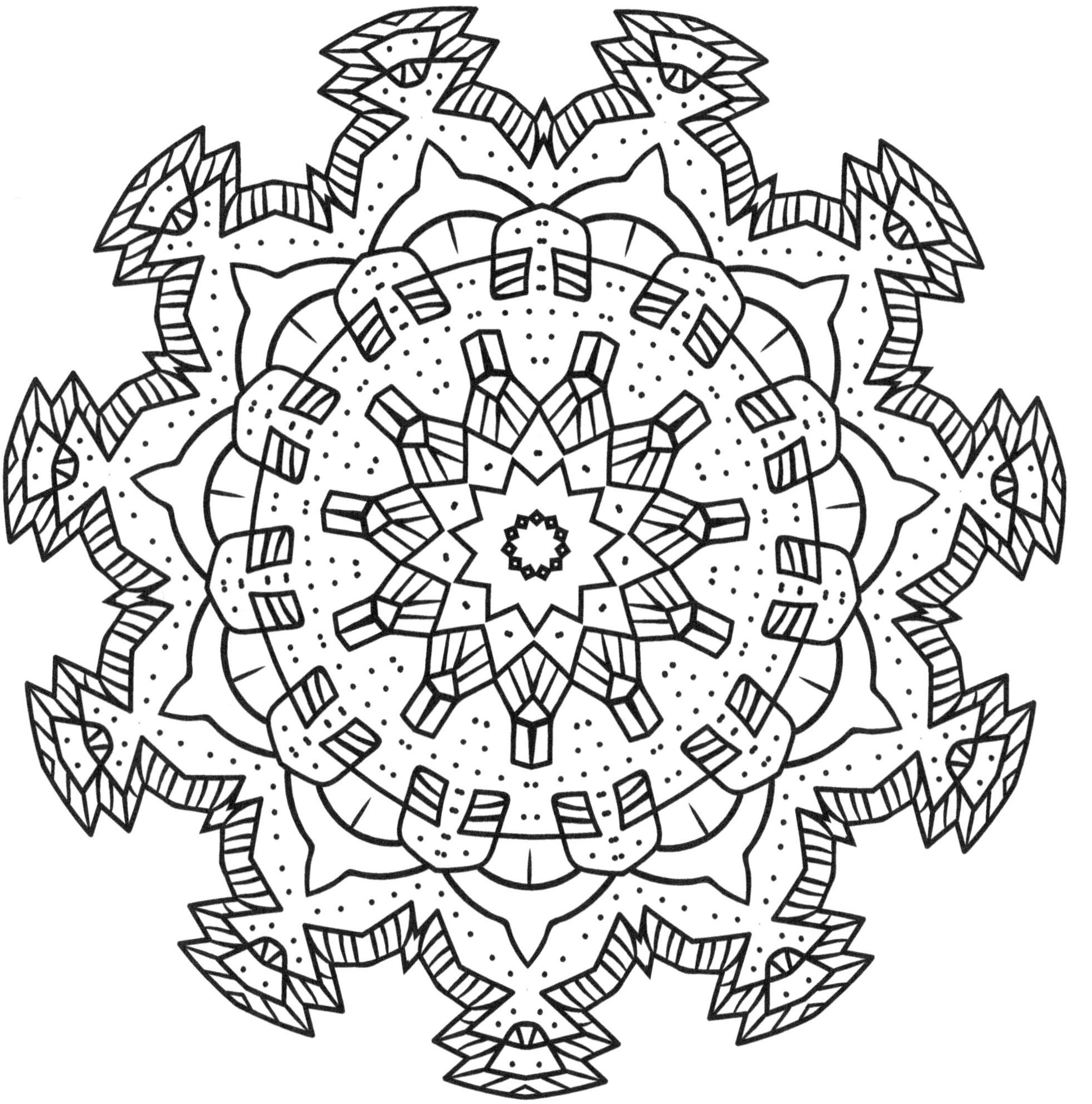

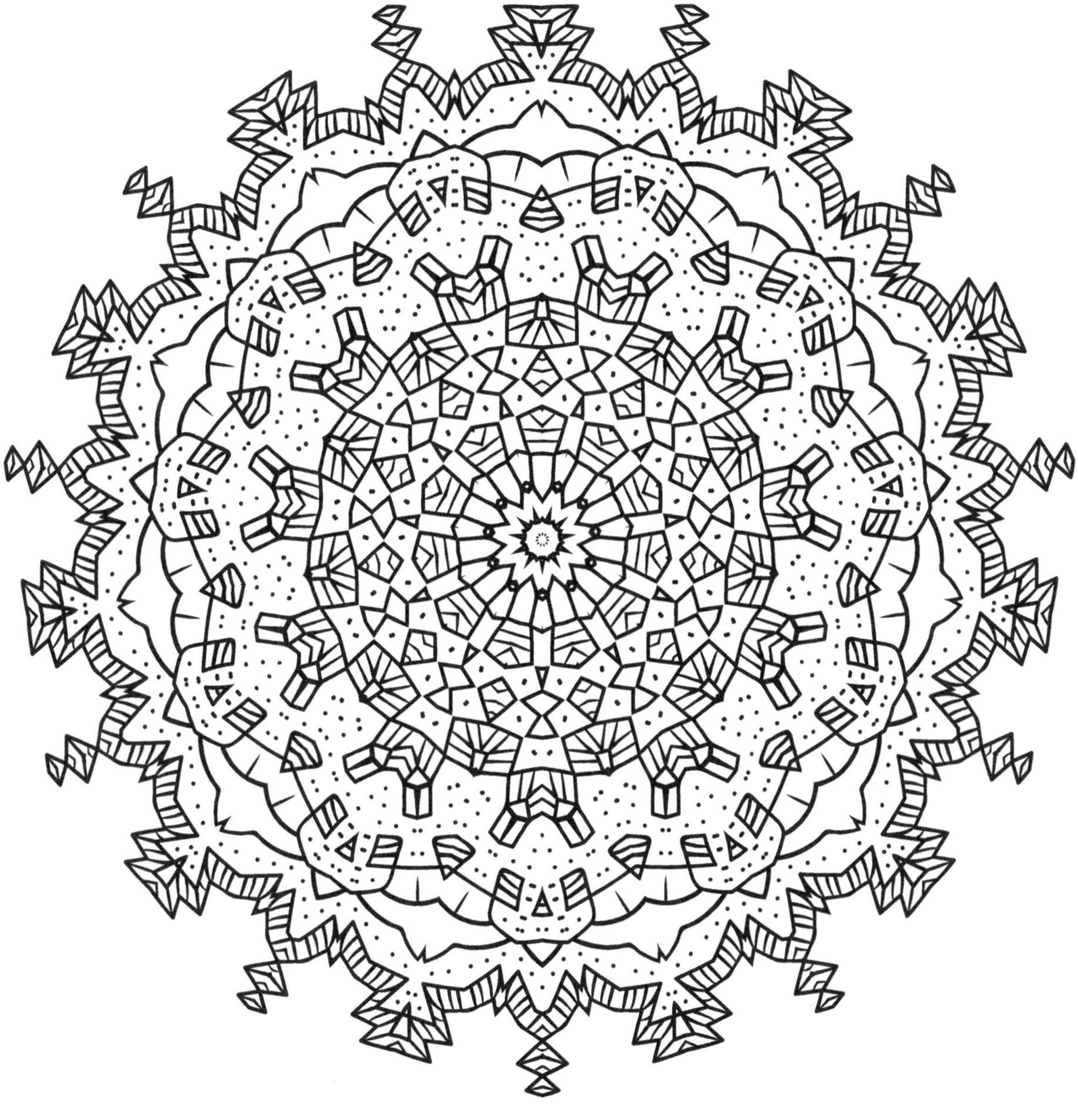

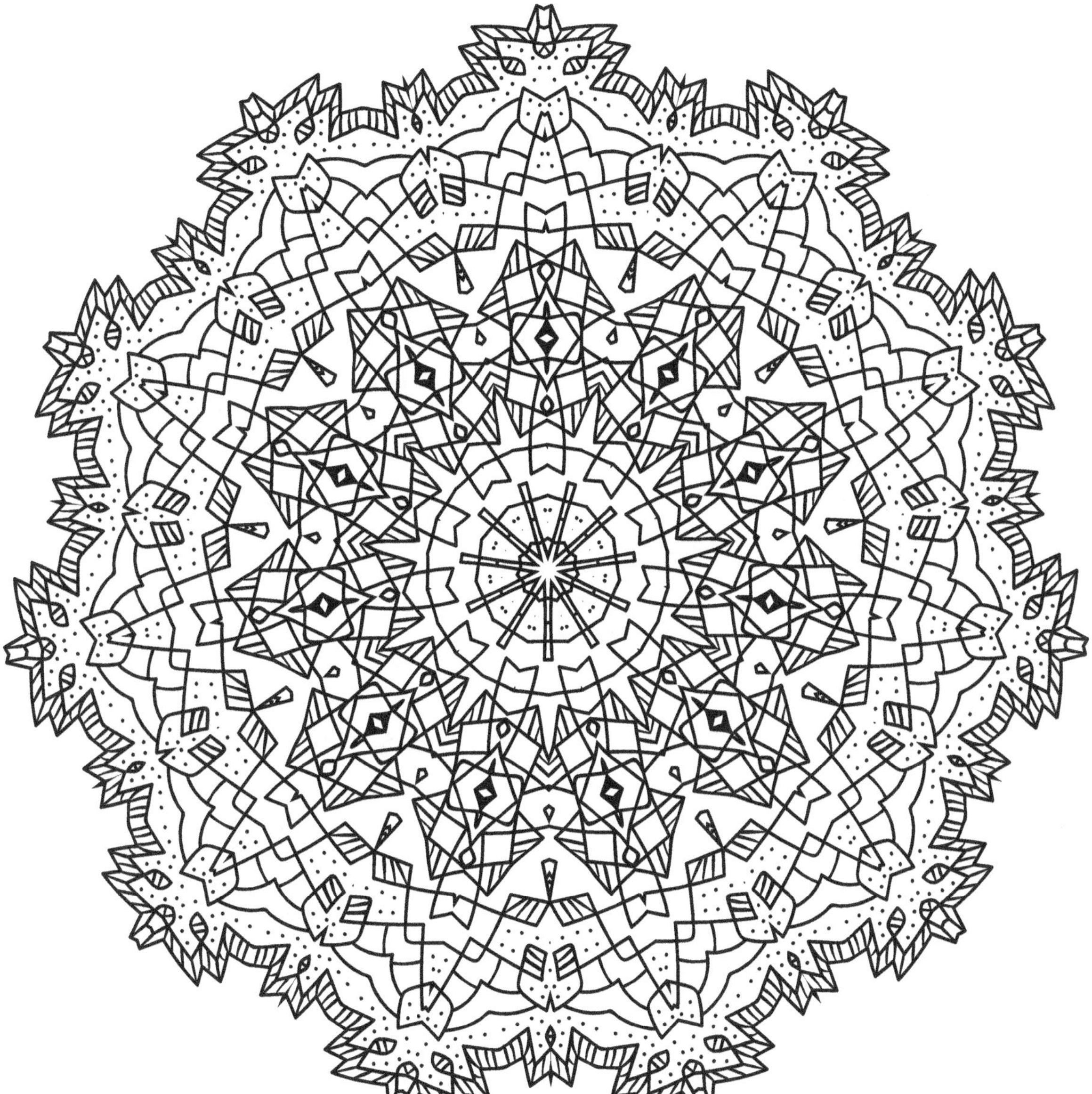

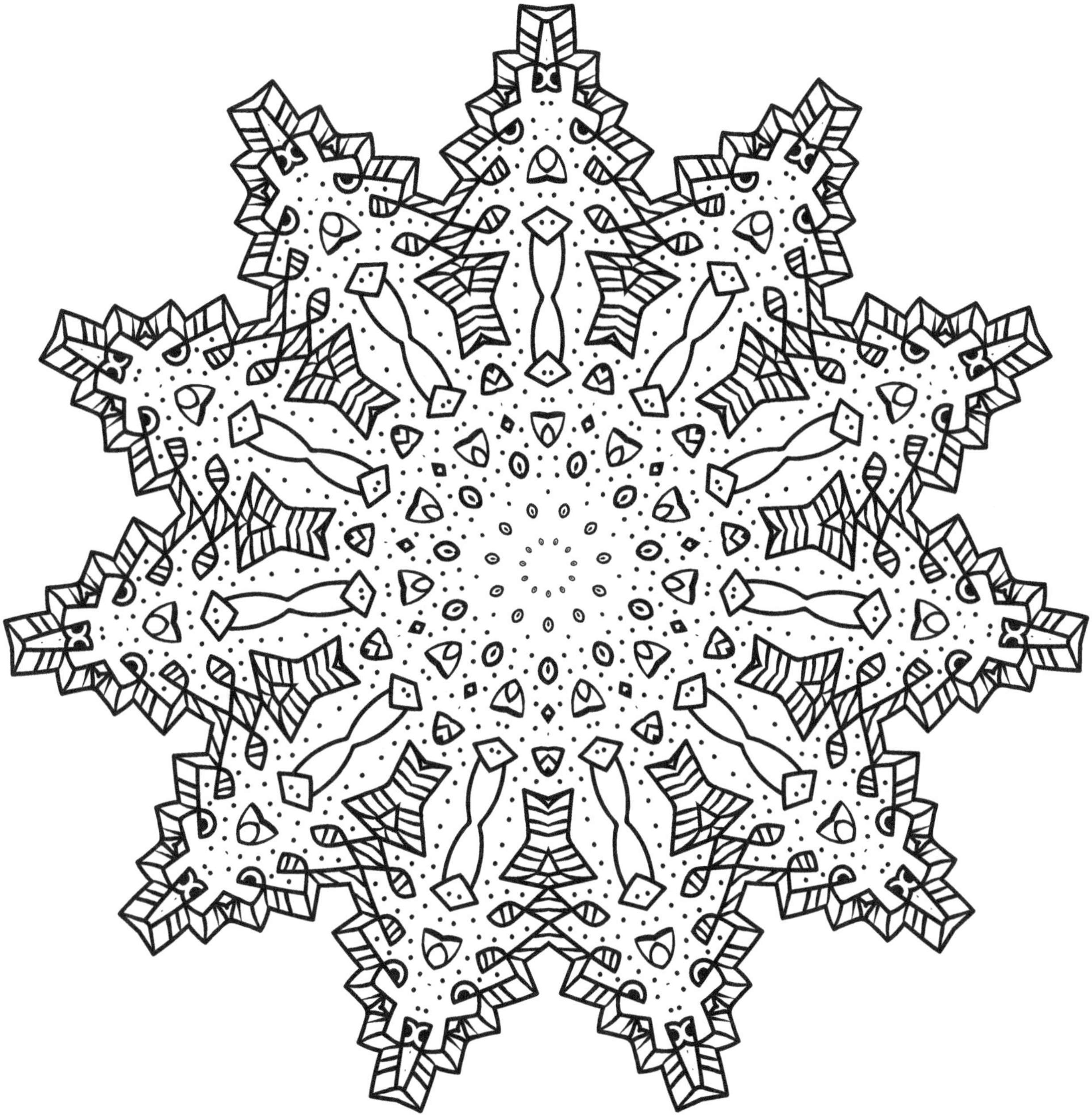

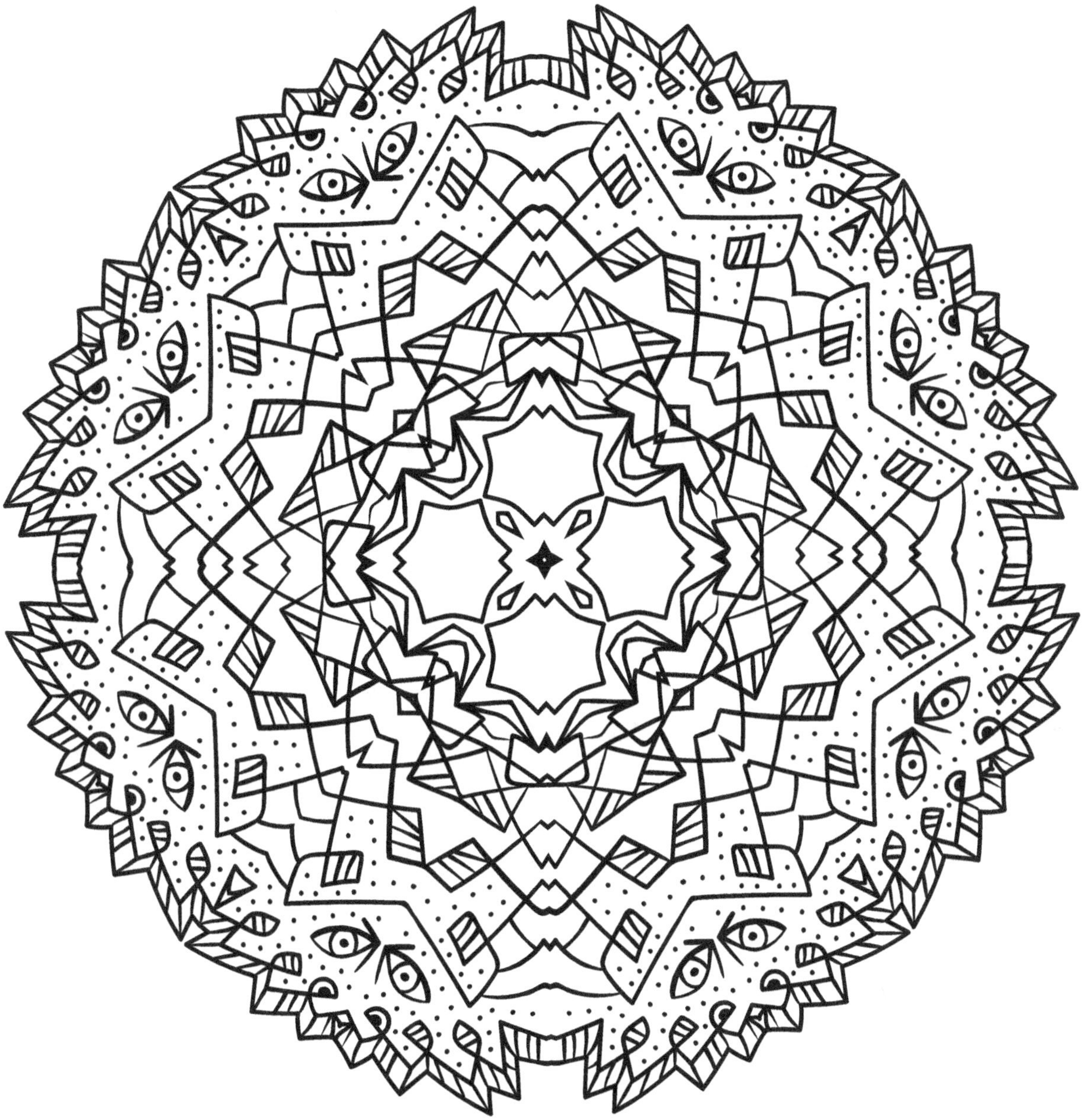

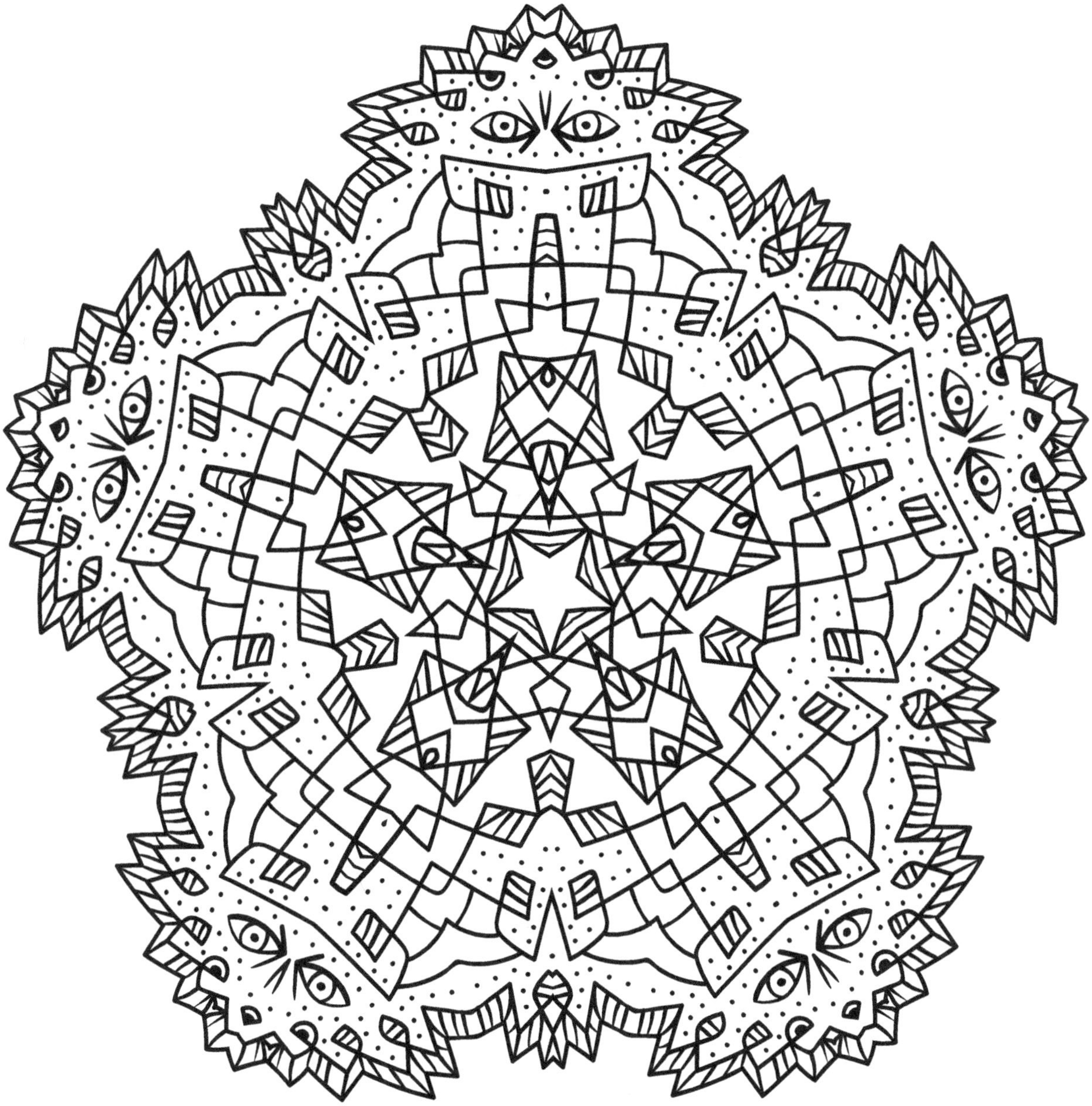

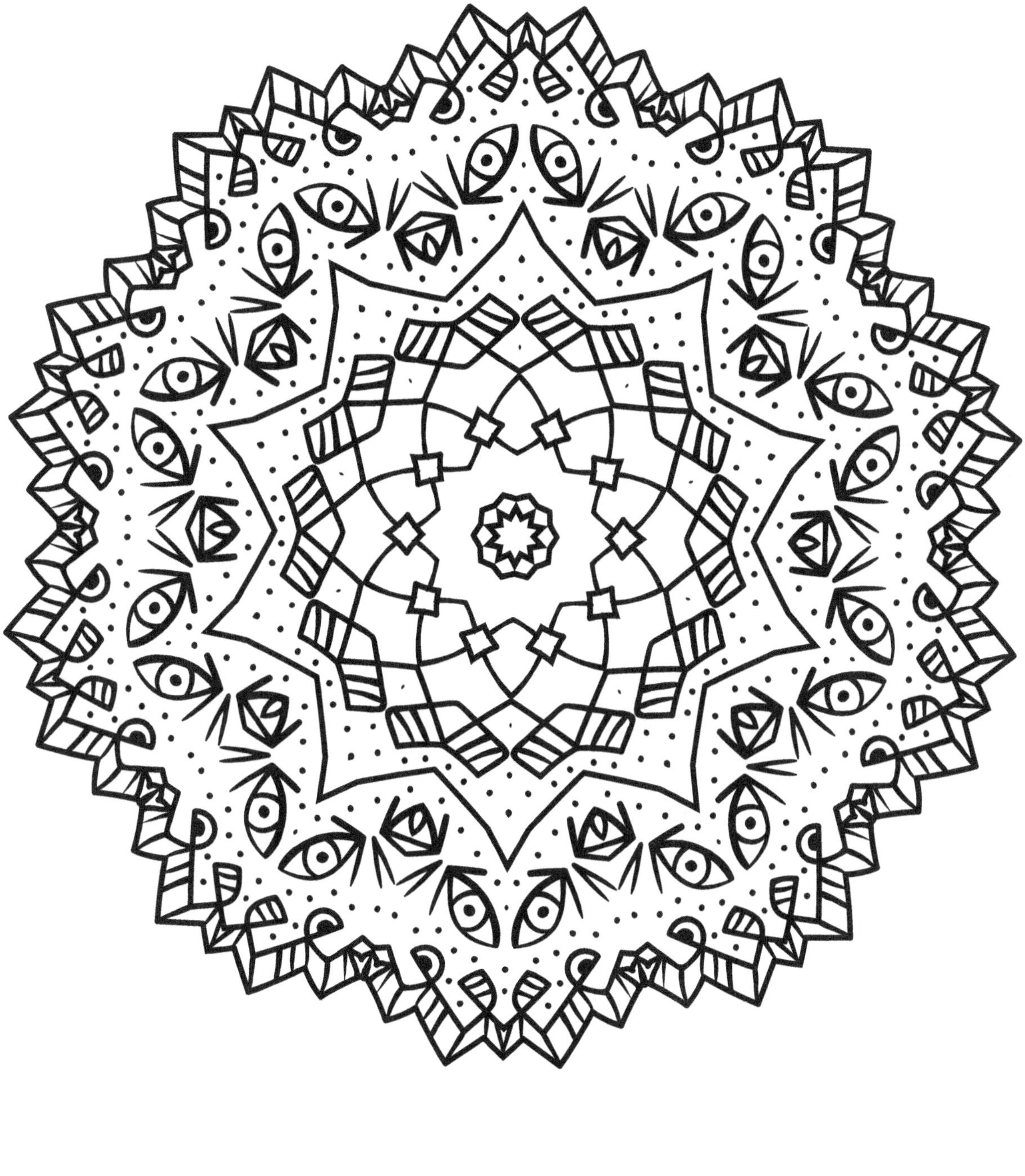

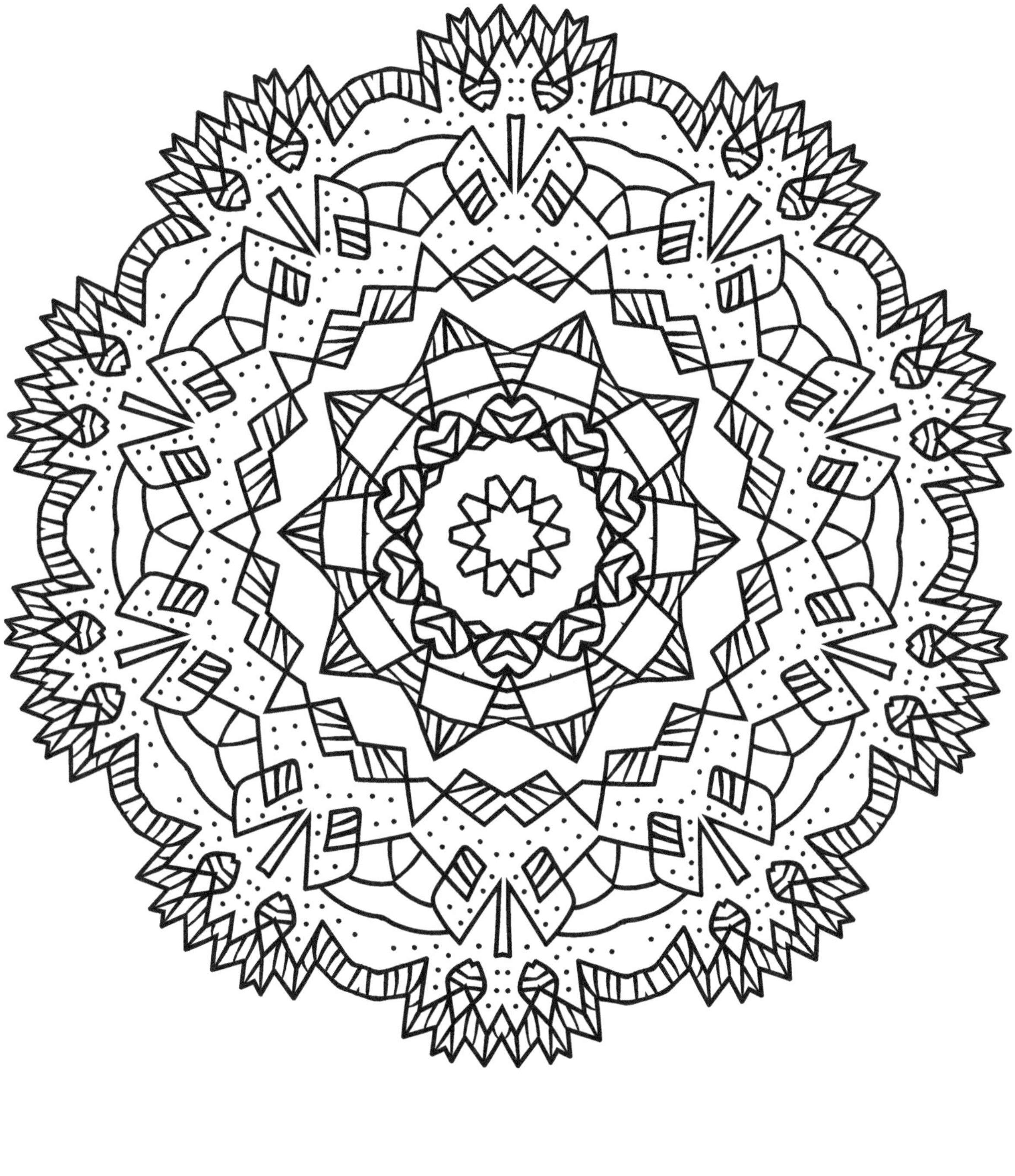

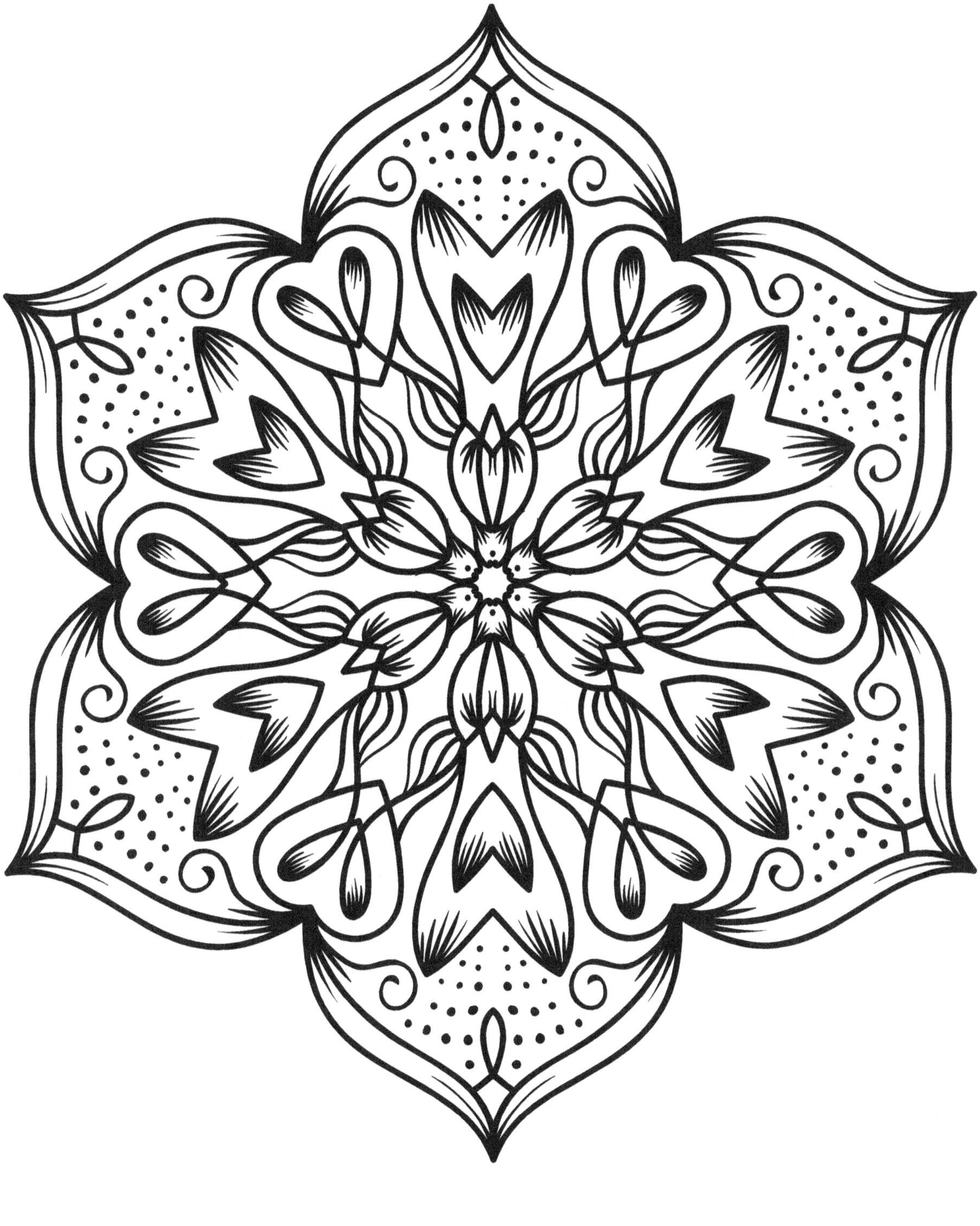

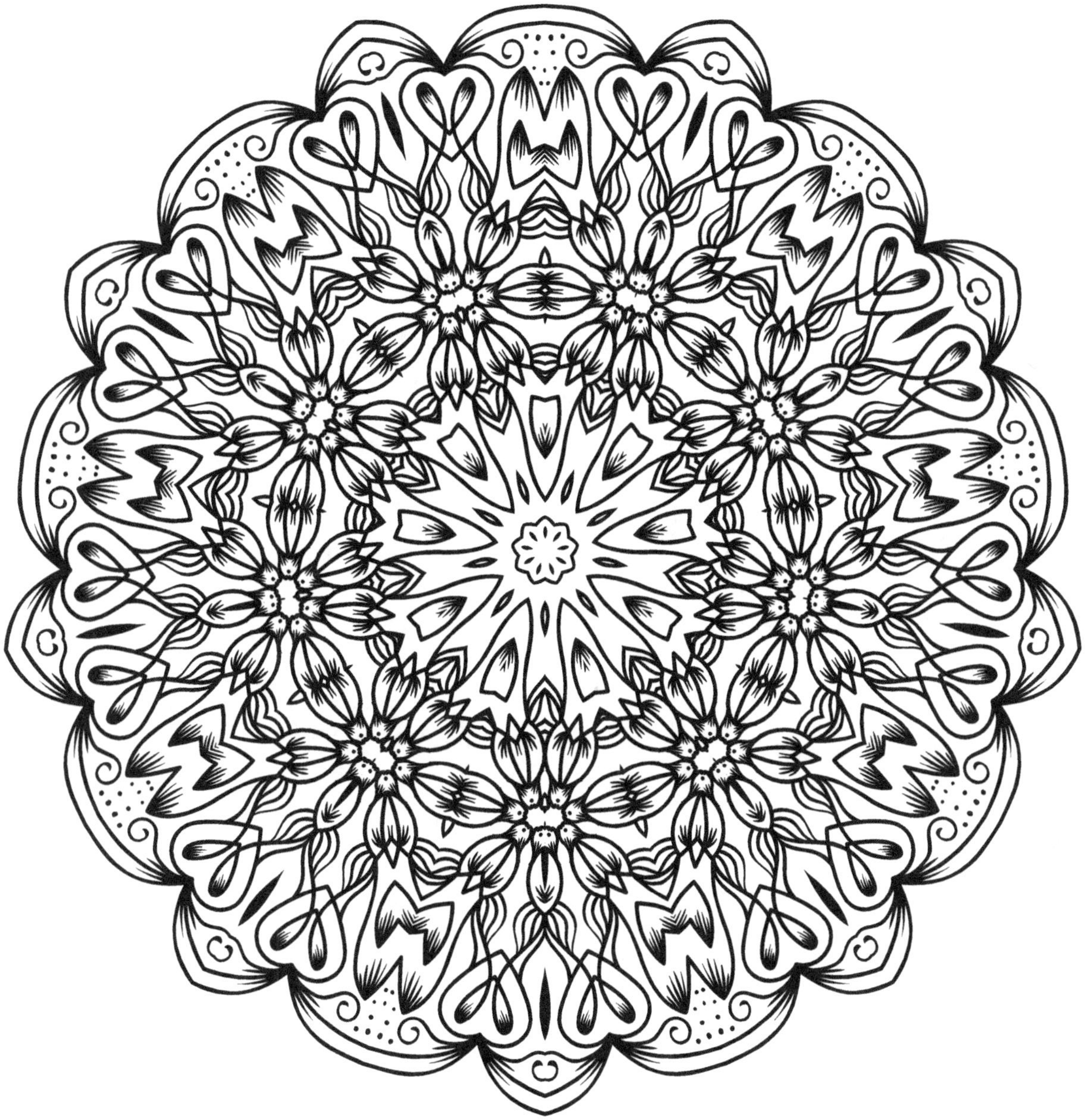

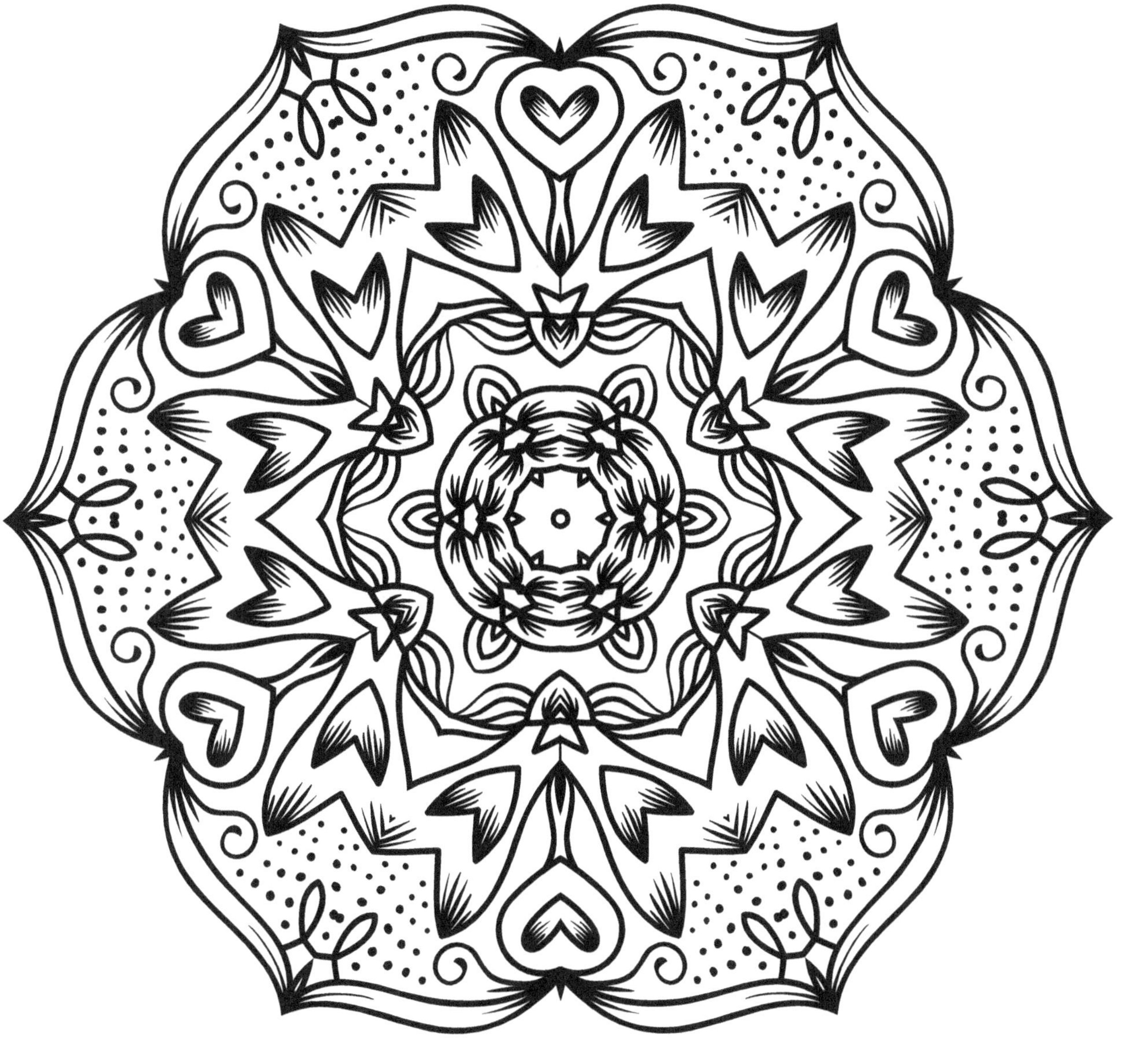

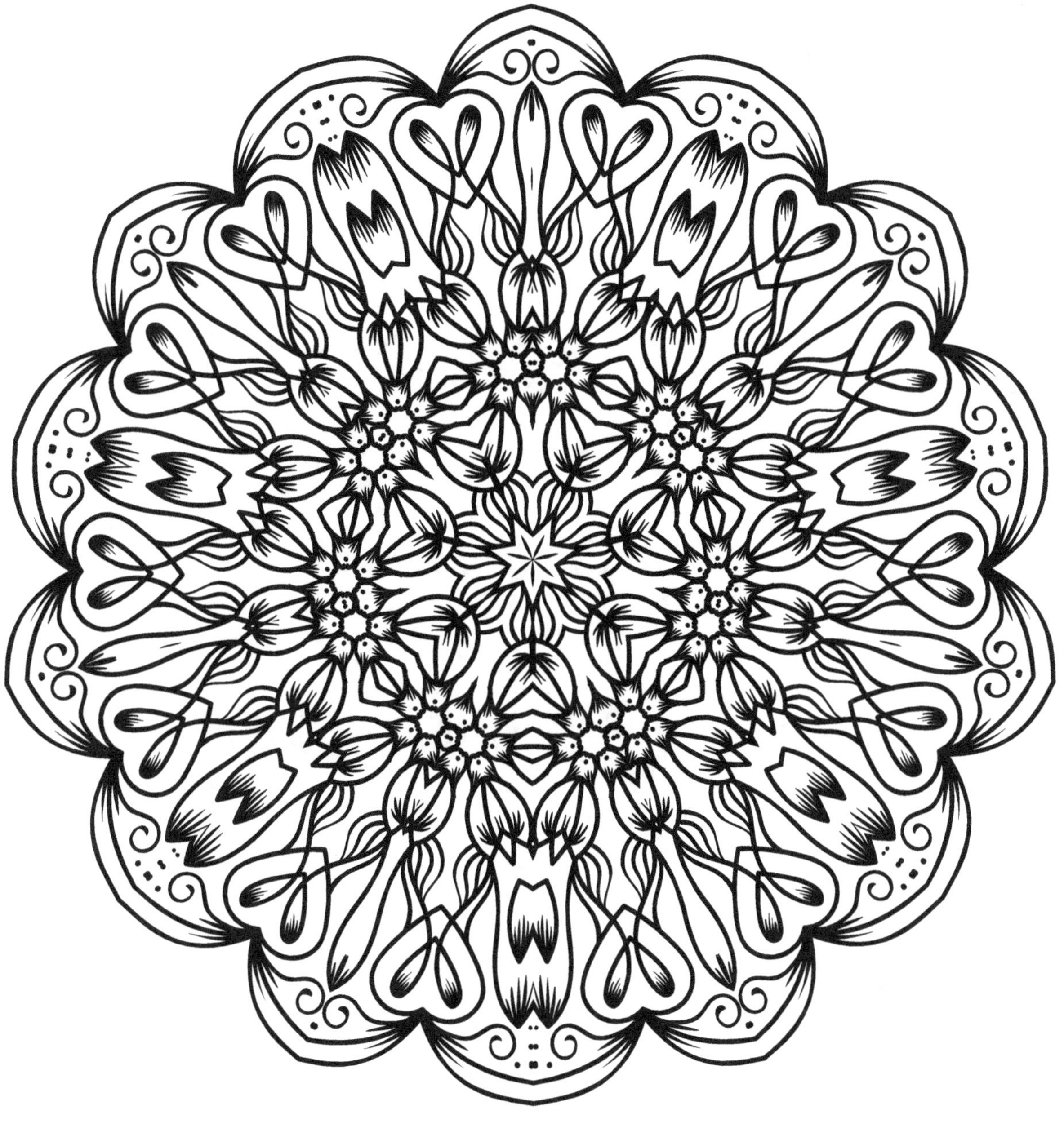

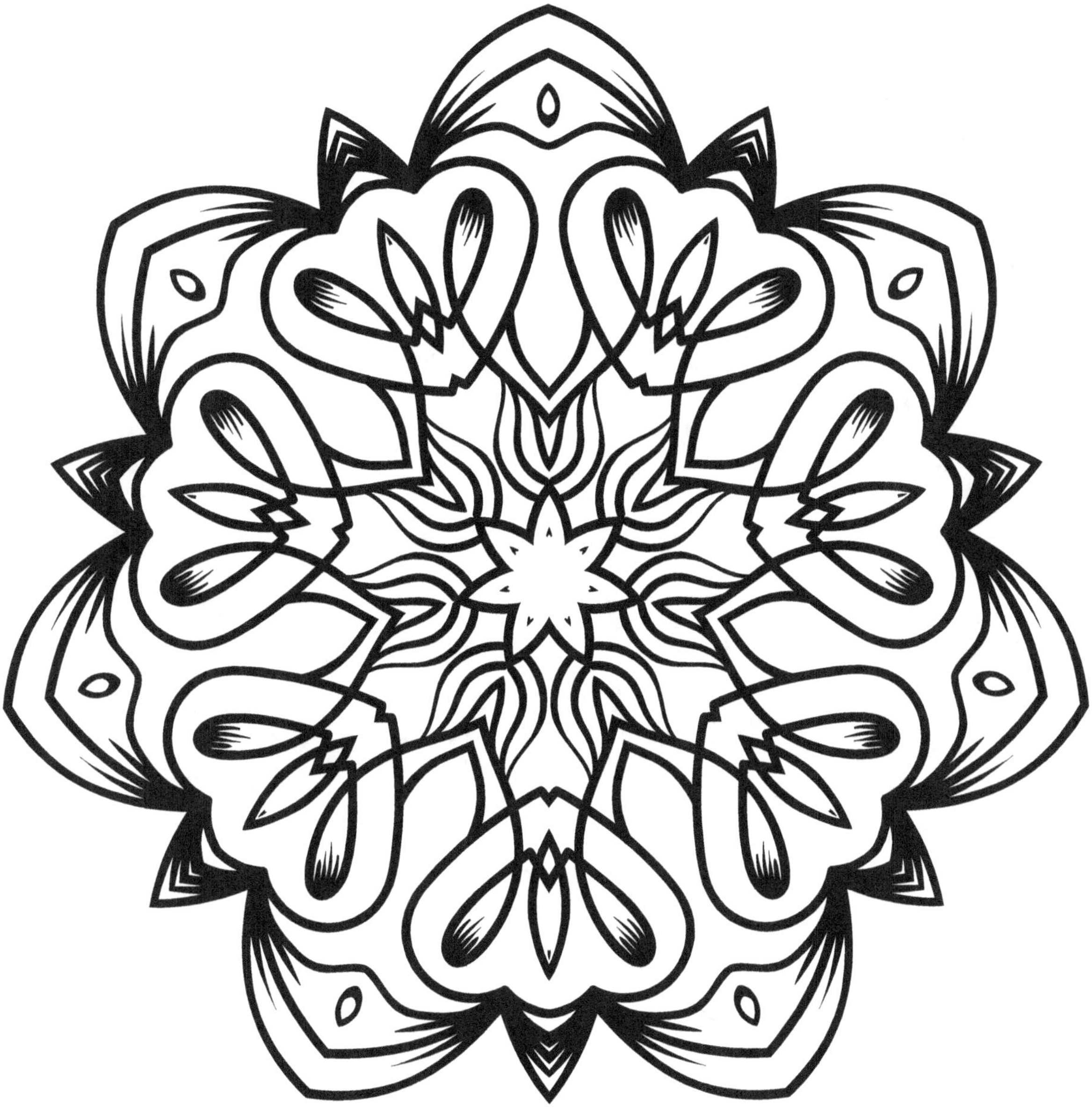

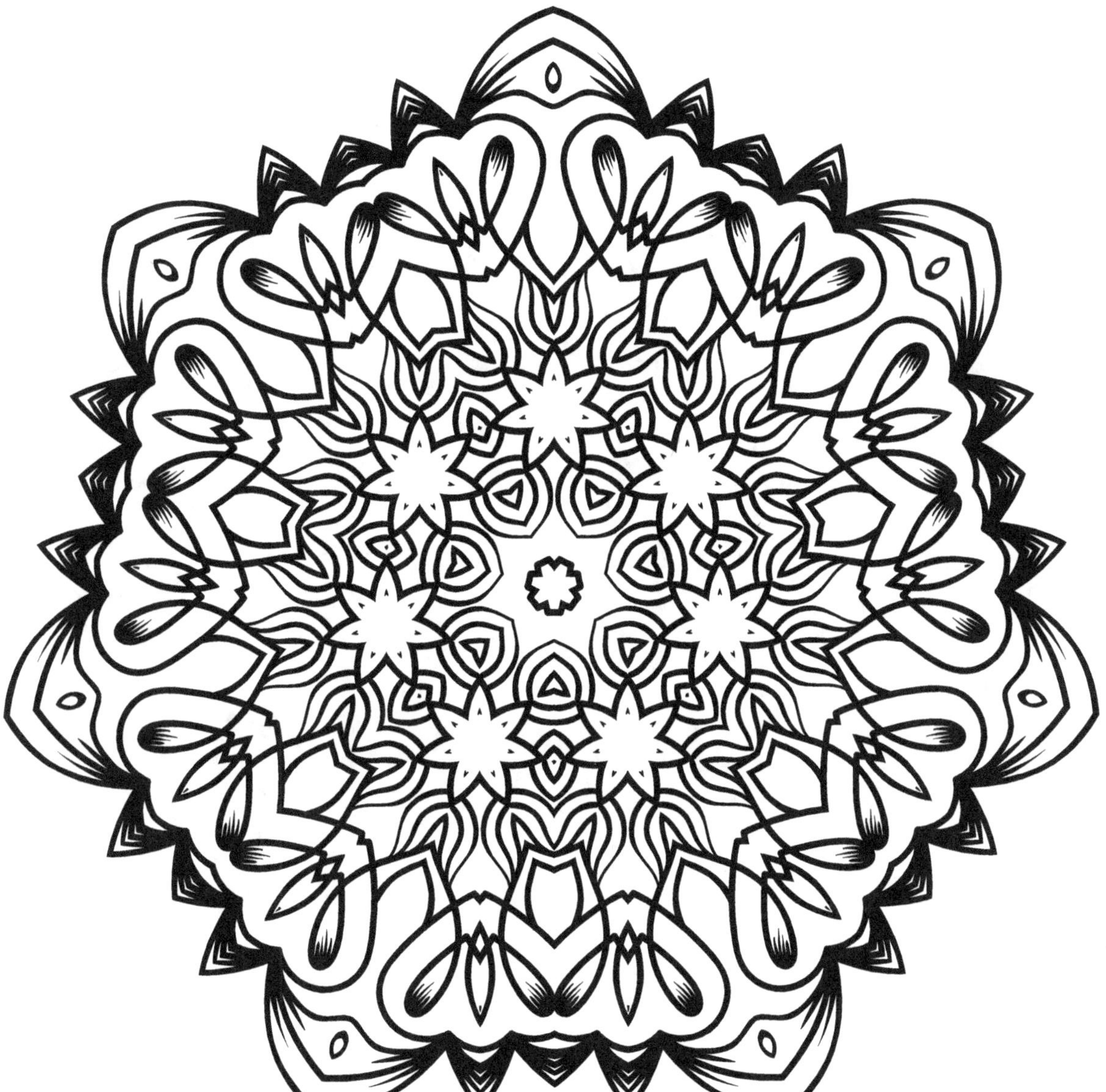

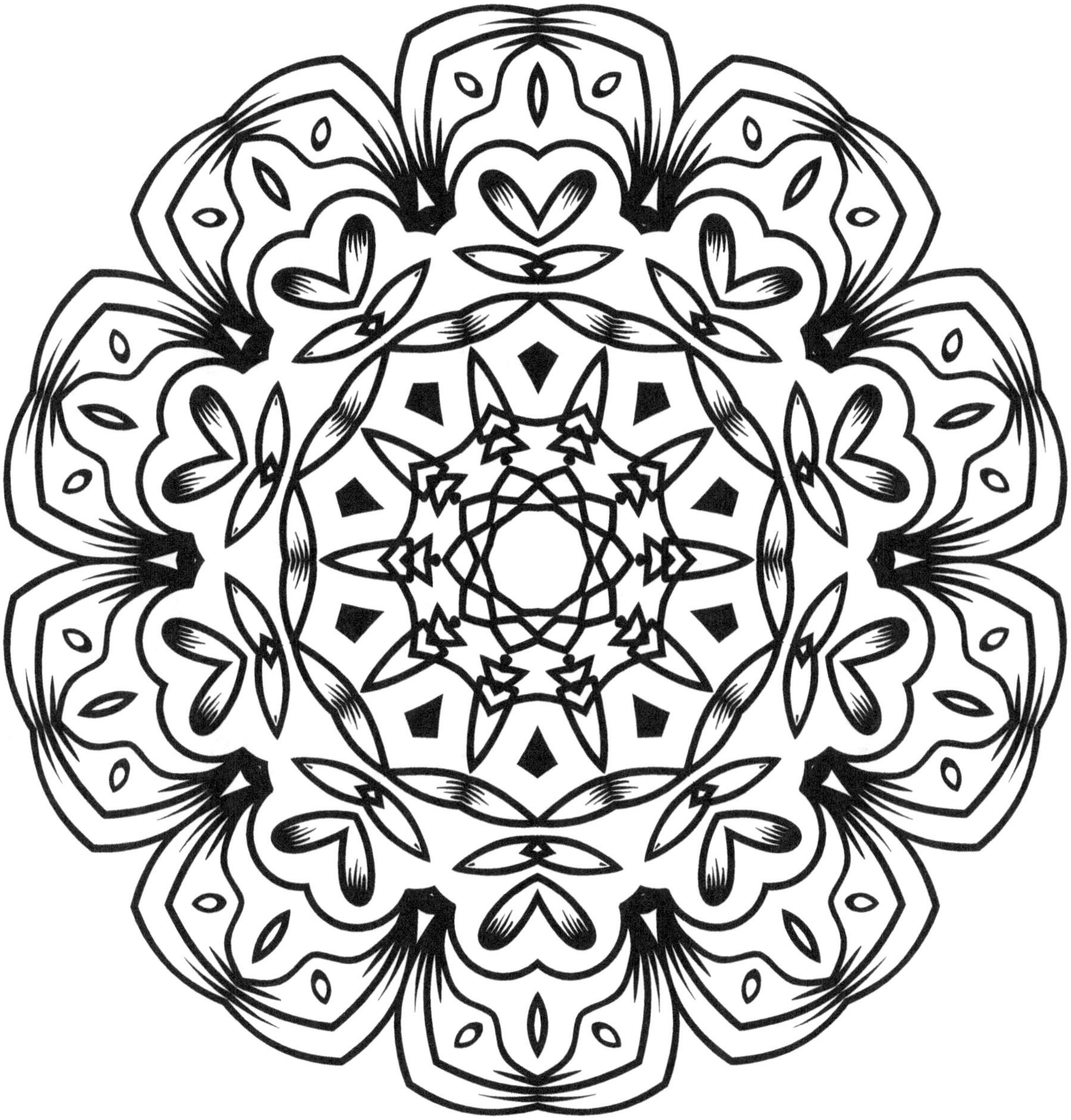

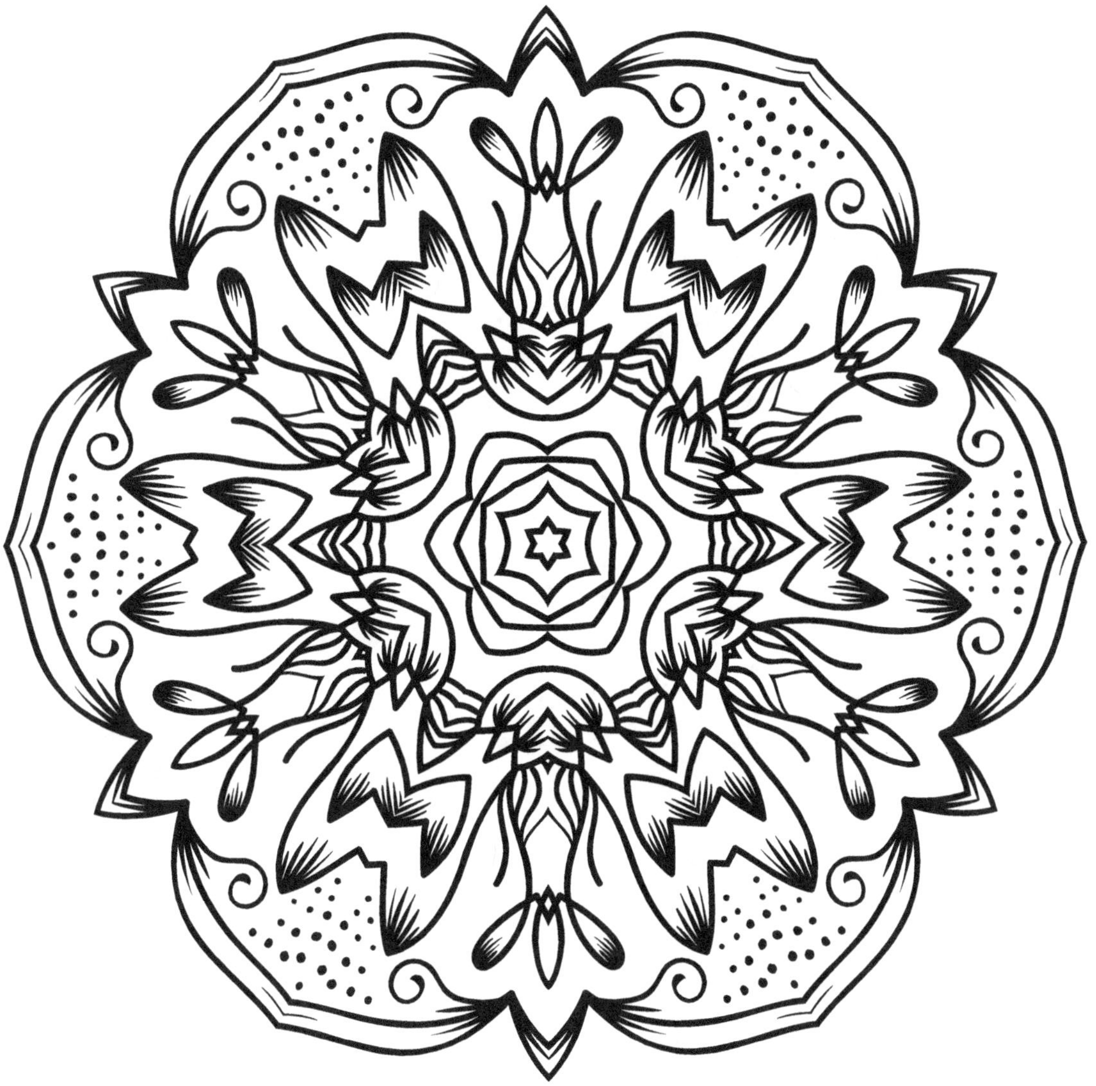

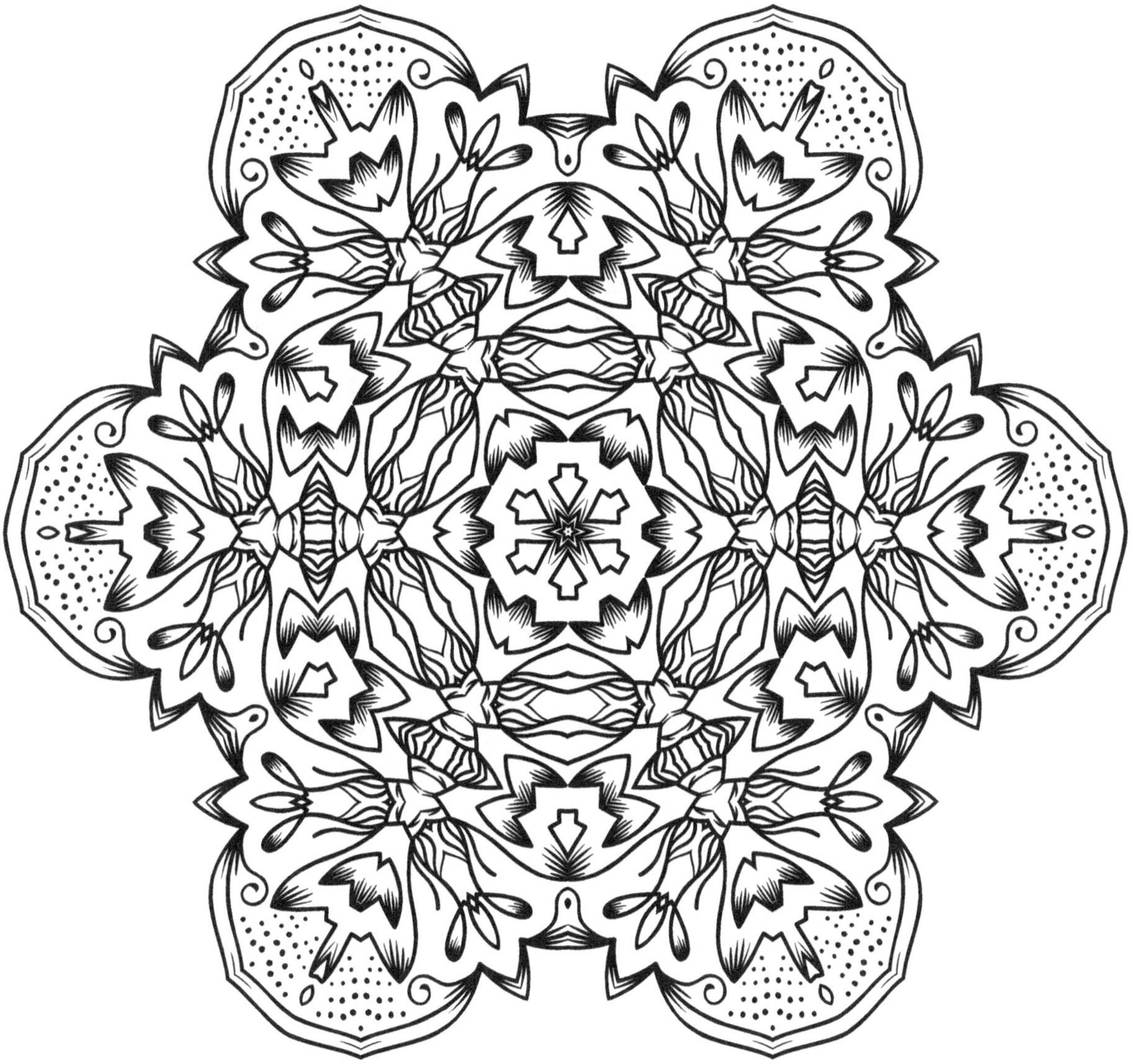

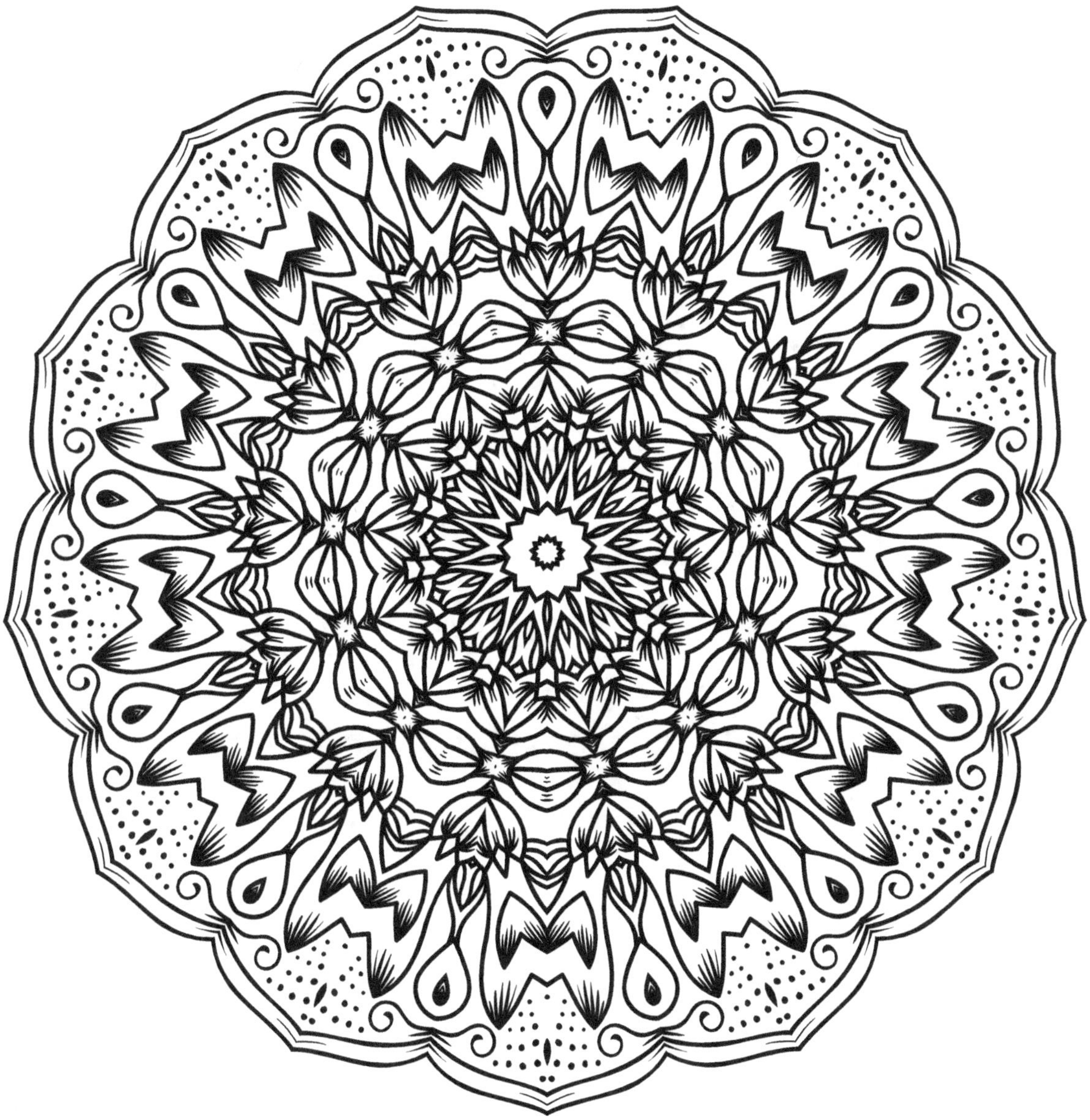

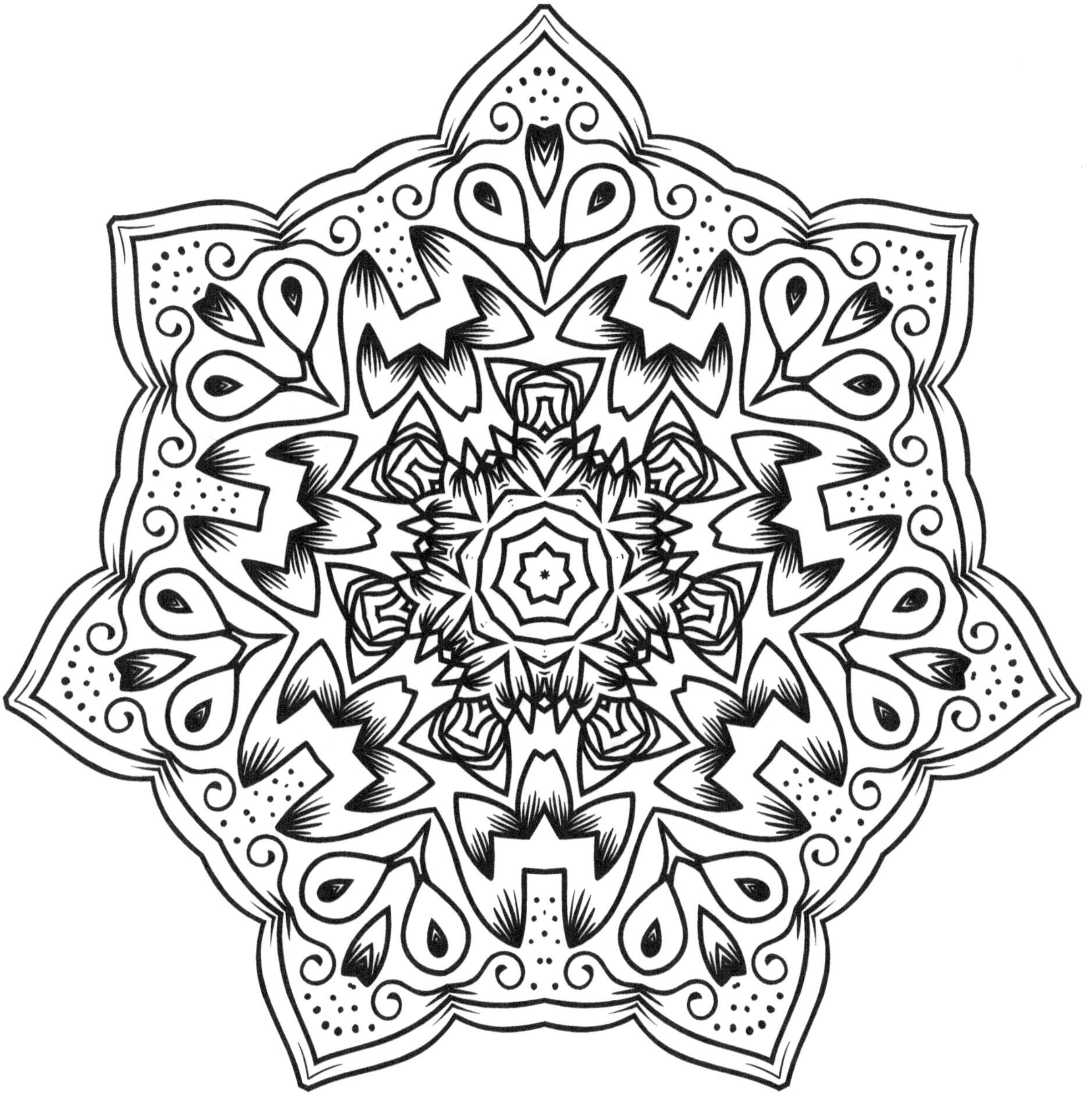

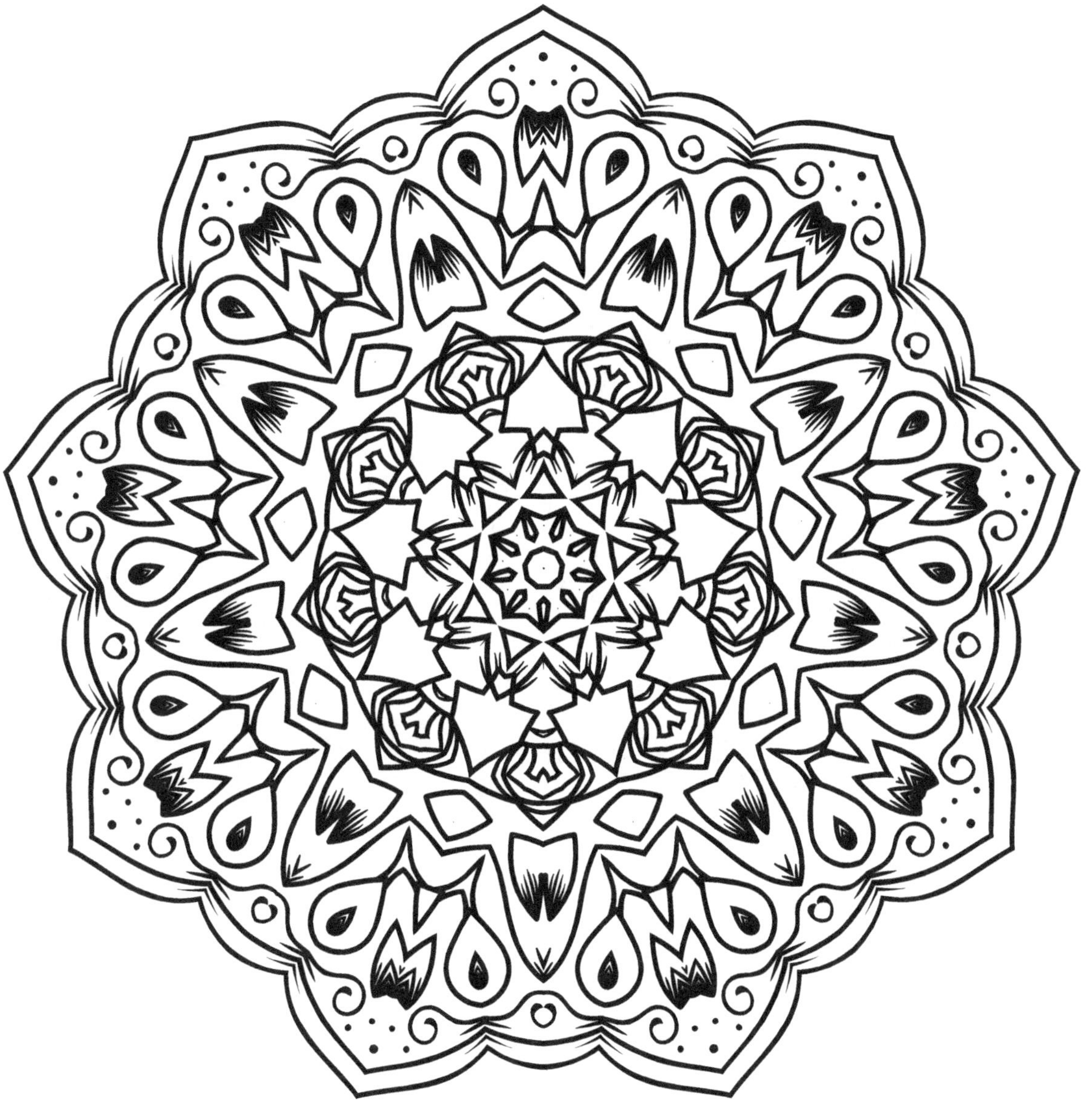

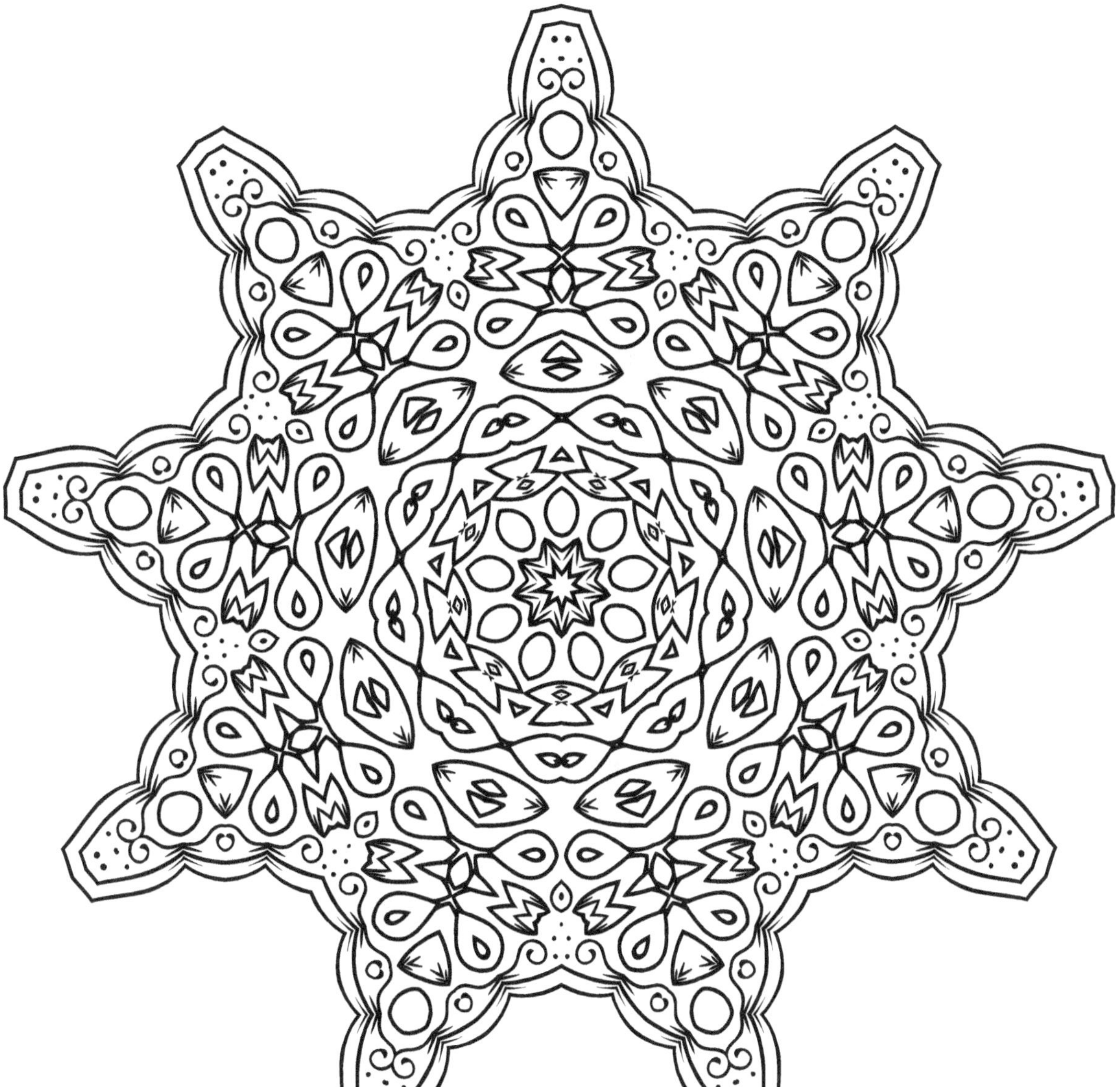

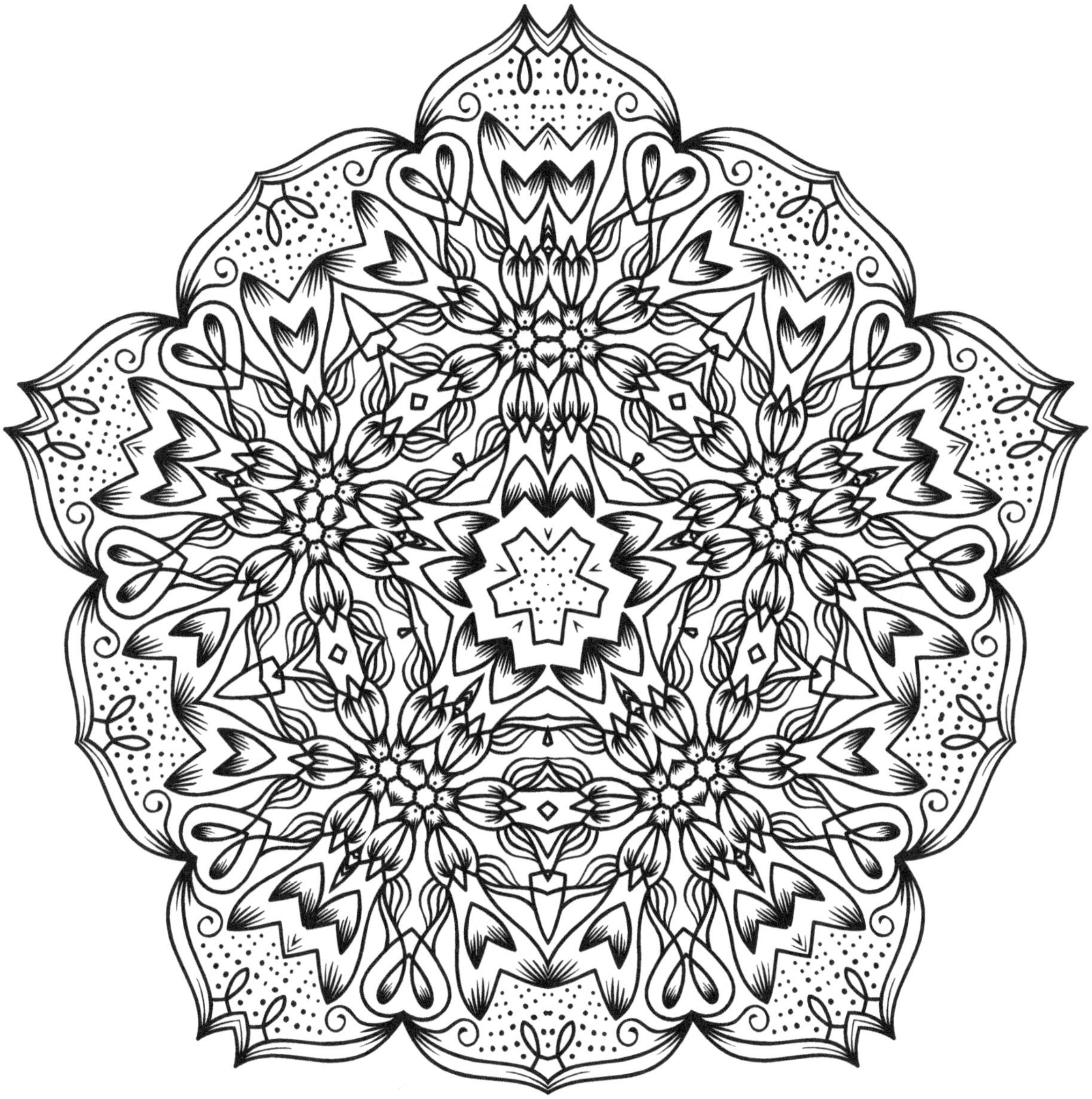

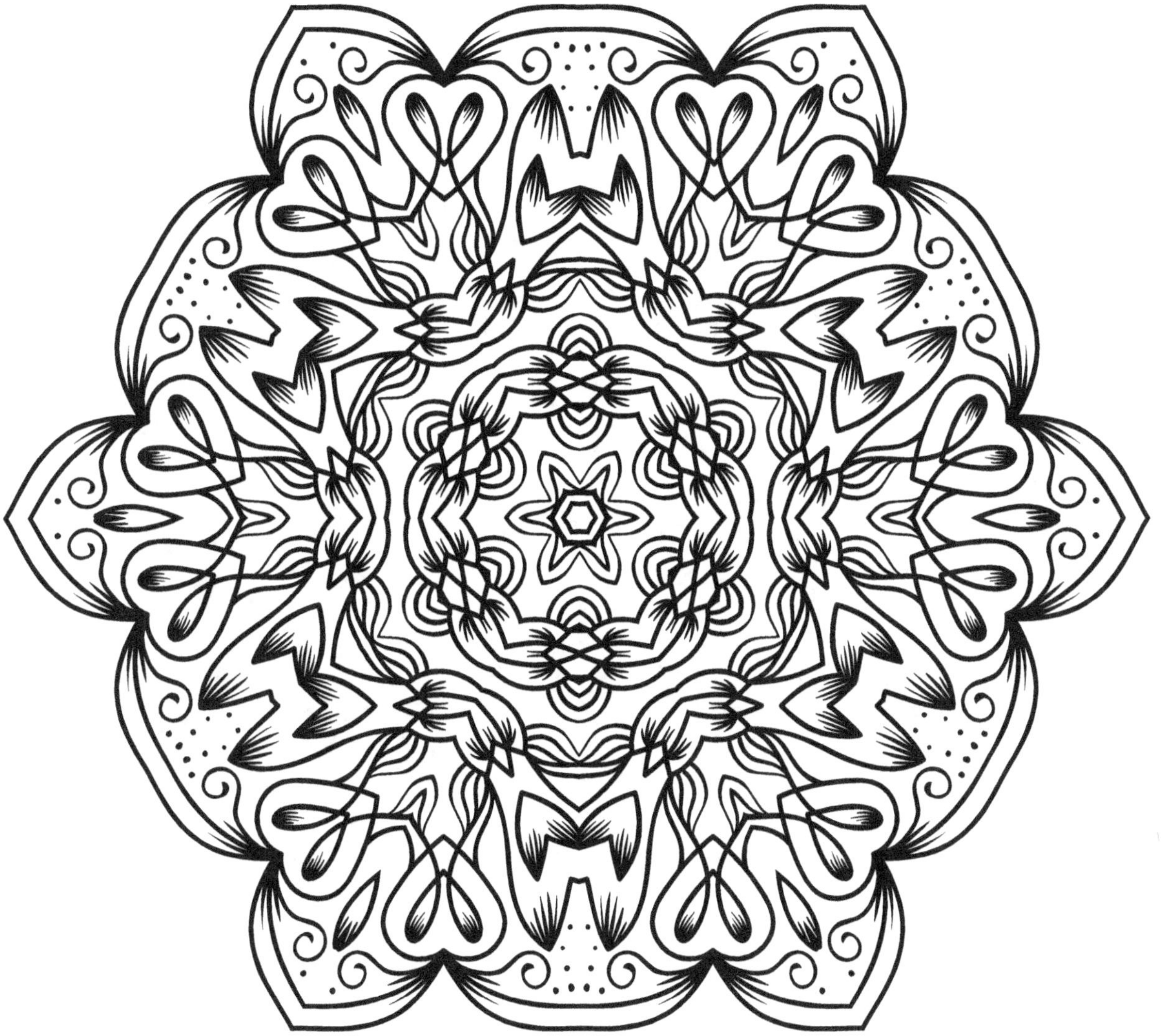

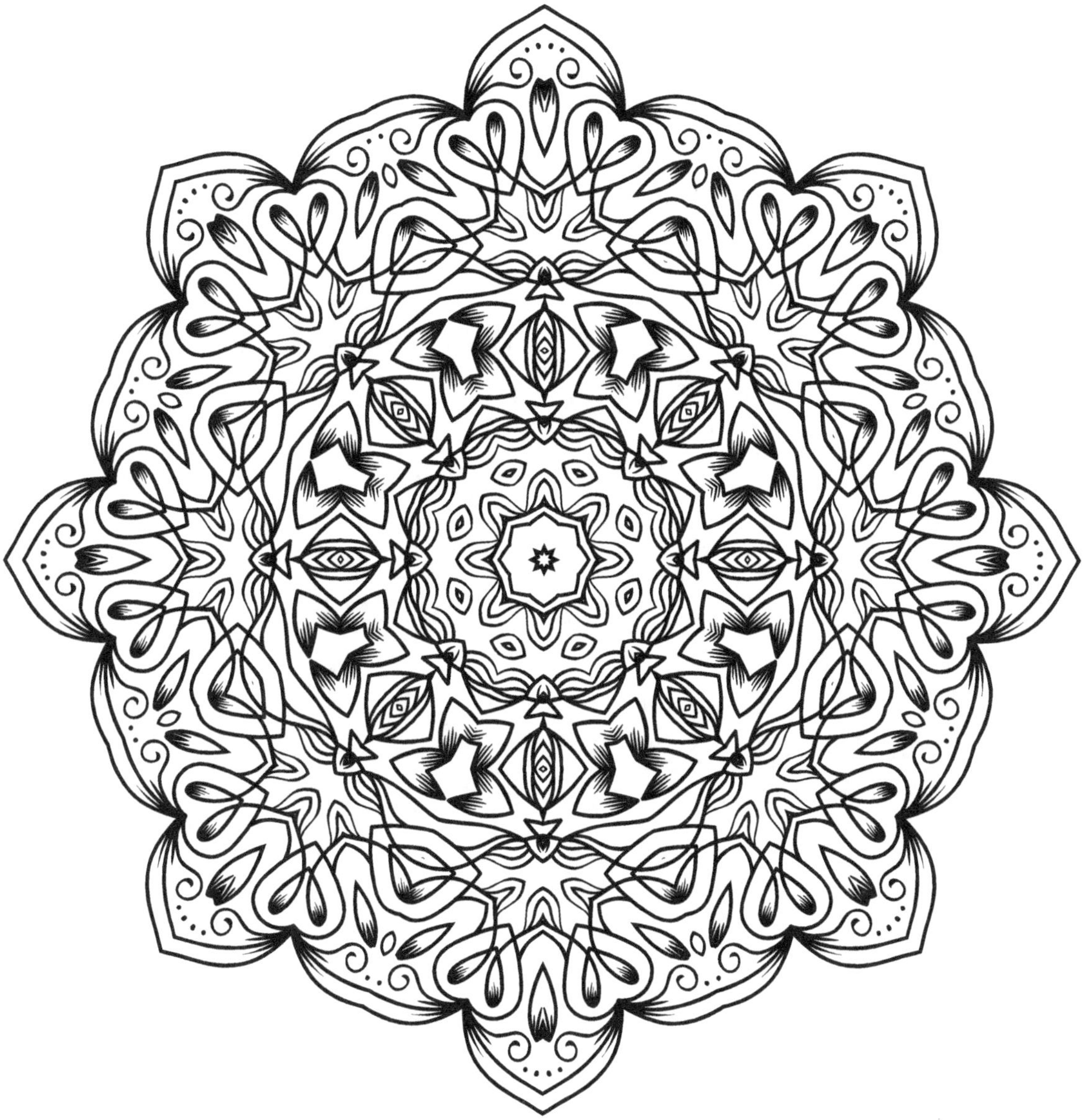

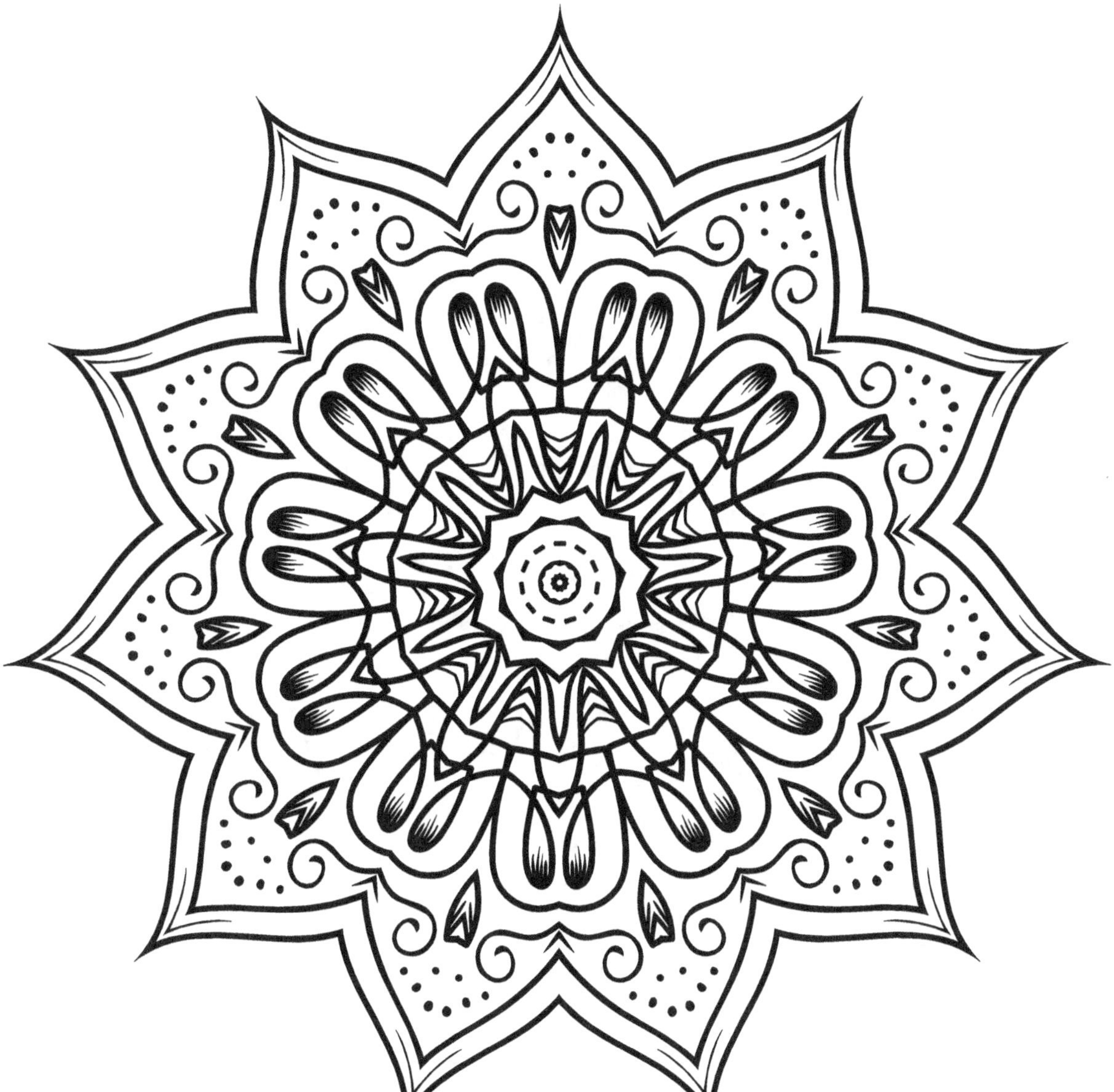

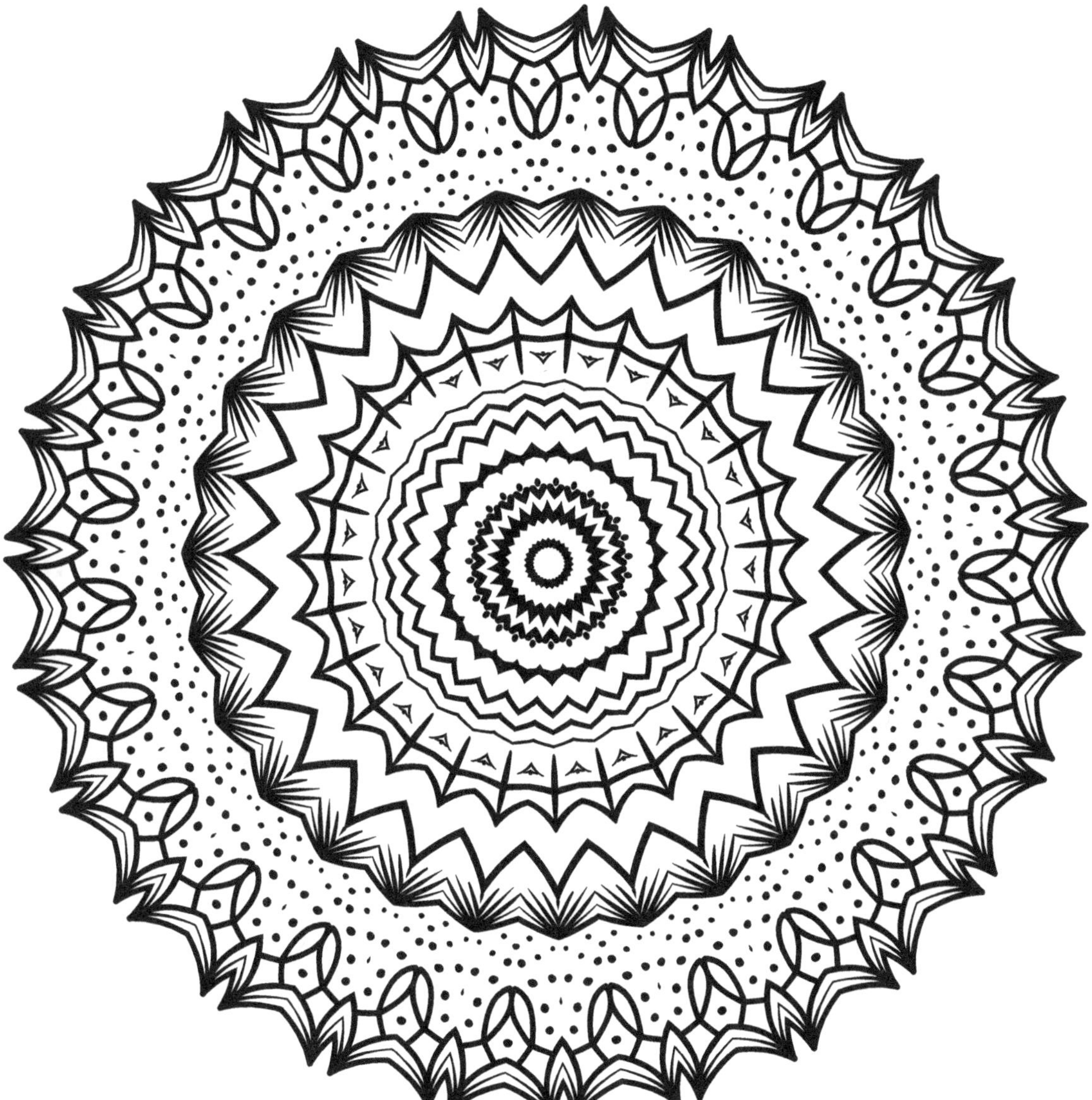

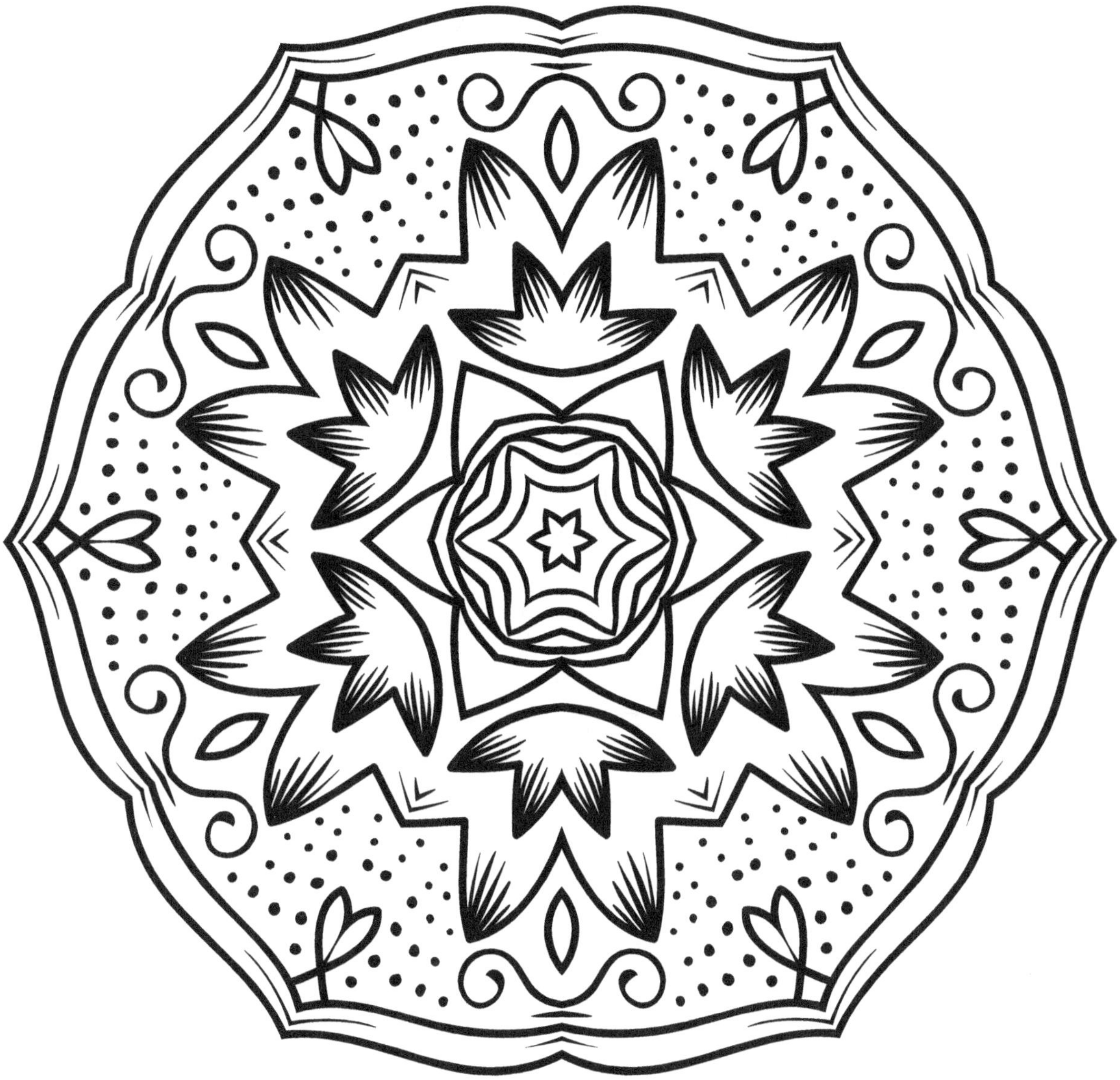

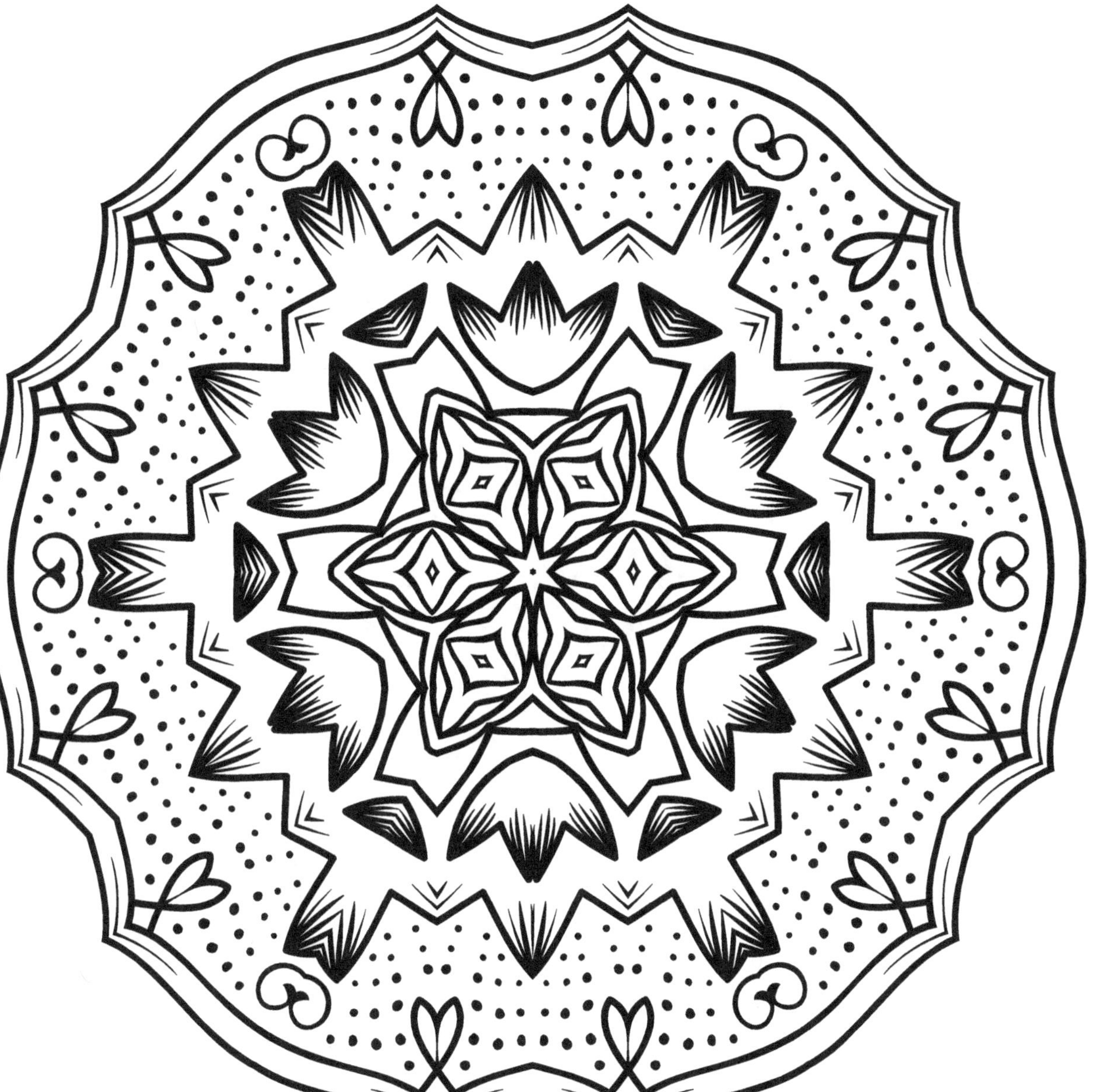

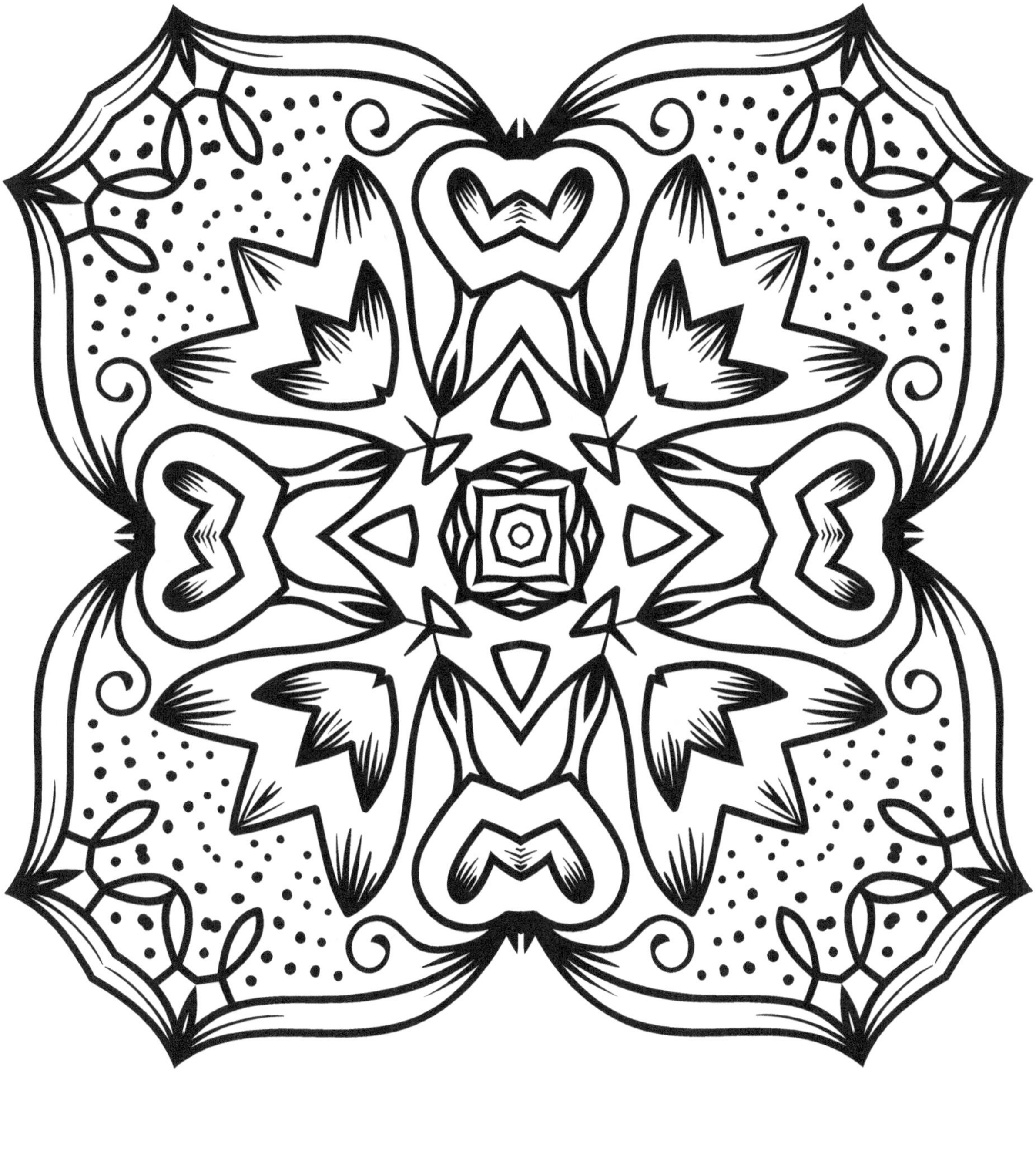

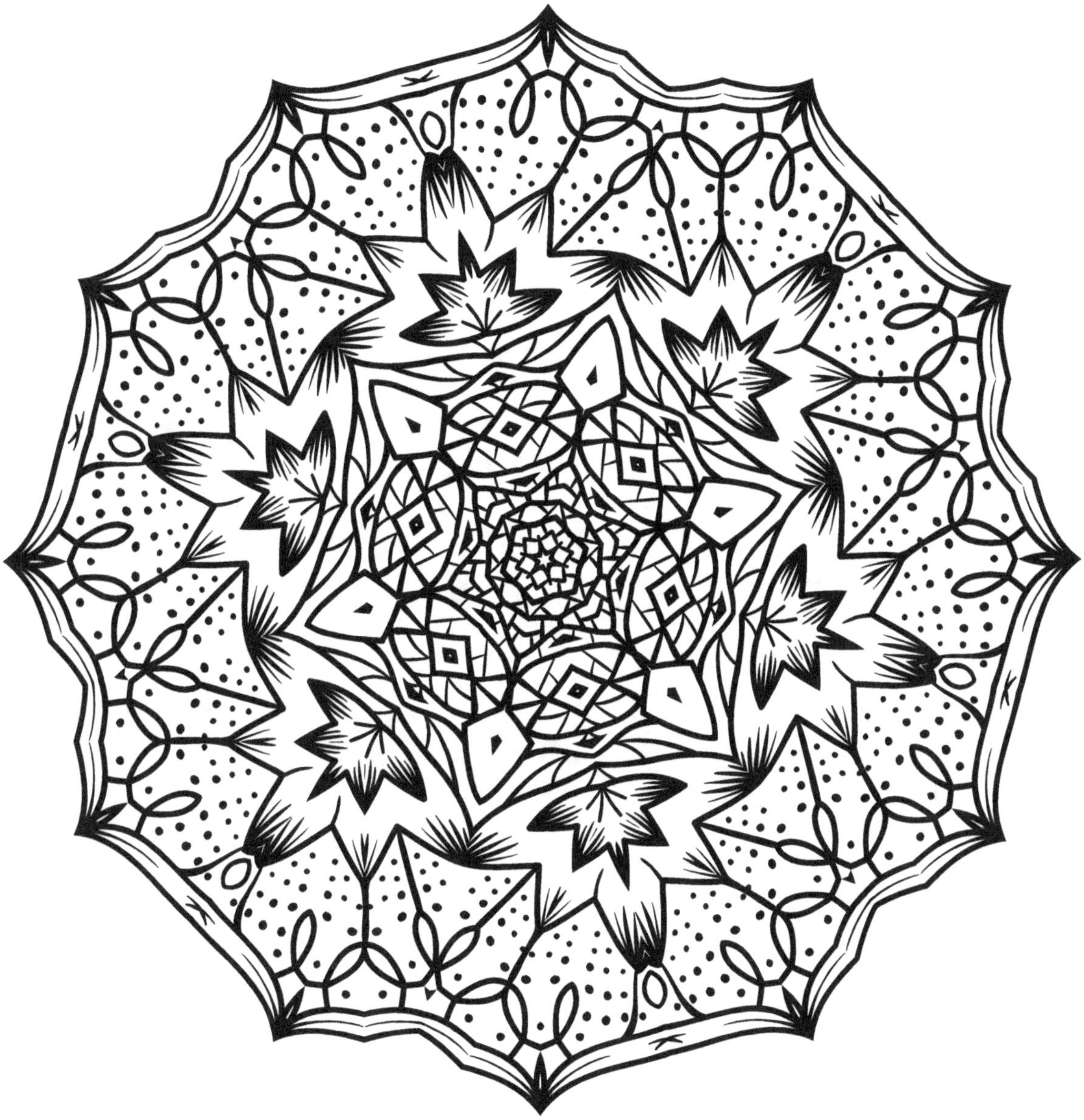

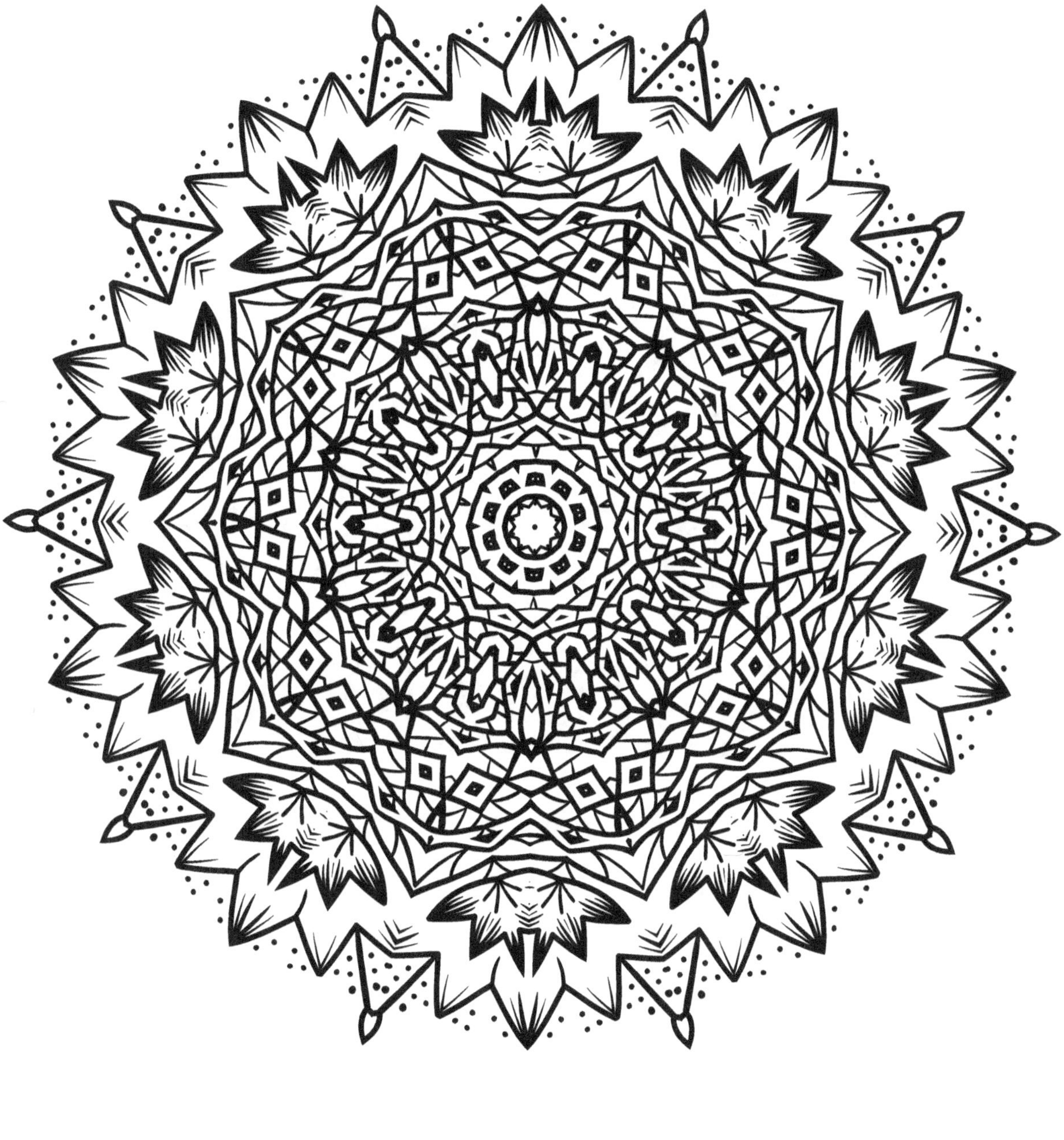

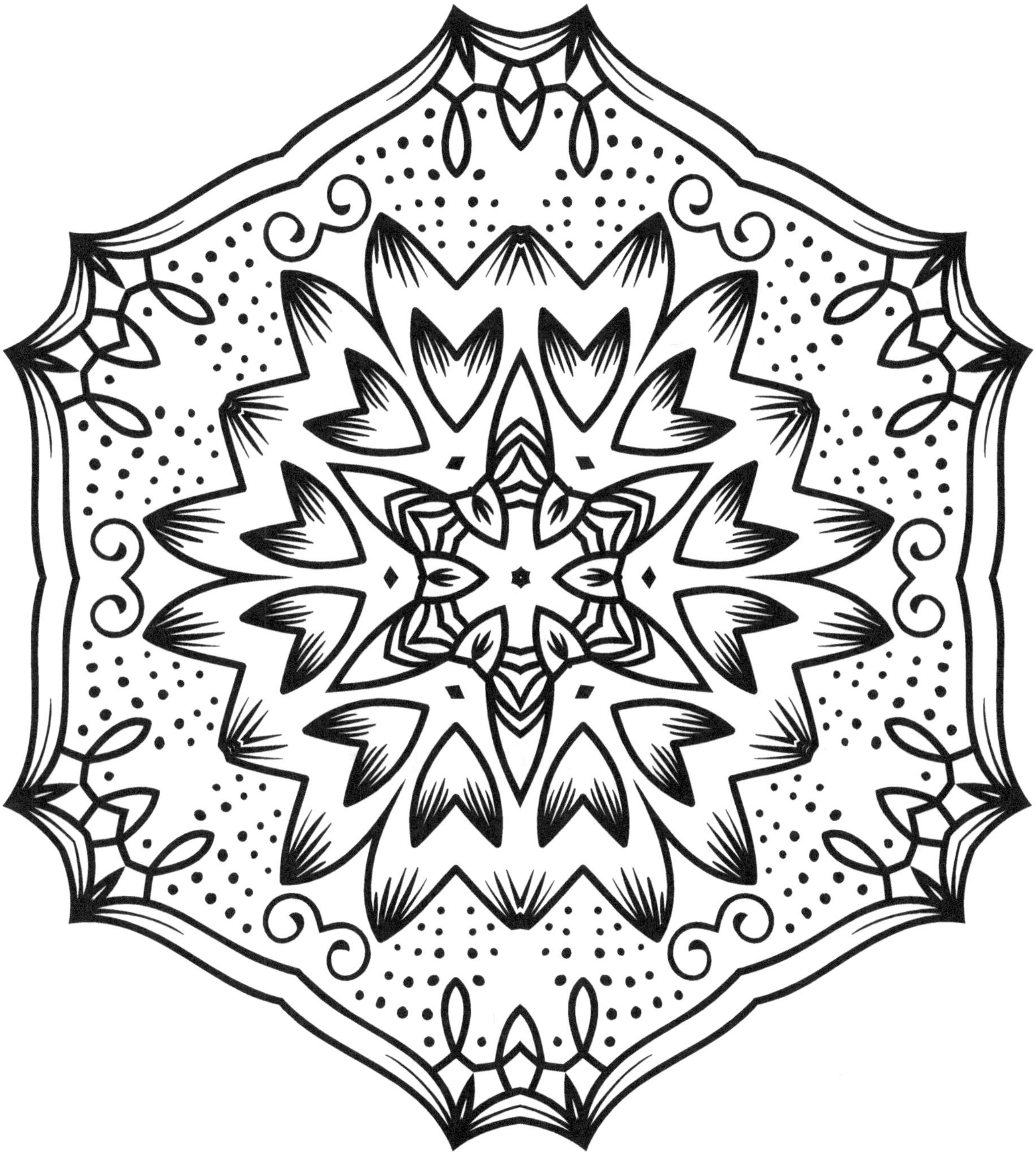

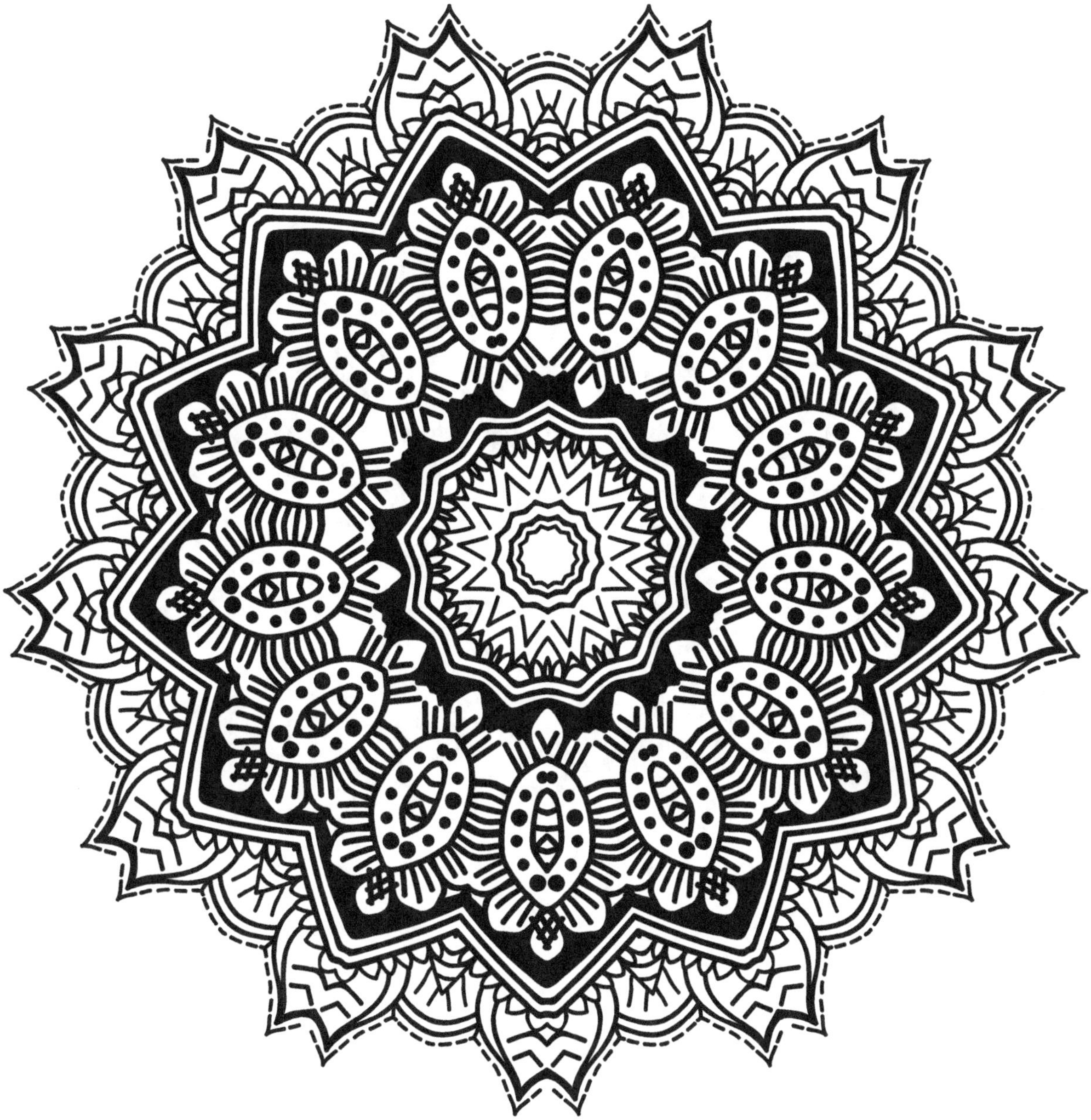

www.ingramcontent.com/pod-product-compliance
Lightning Source LLC
Chambersburg PA
CBHW082146230526
45467CB00043B/2364
9798704728900